CREATIVE WAYS
TO PRAY

Ideas for Individuals,

Small Groups

and Prayer Gatherings

PAUL COVERT

PrayerShop
Publishing

Terre Haute, Indiana

PrayerShop Publishing is the publishing arm of the Church Prayer Leaders Network. The Church Prayer Leaders Network exists to equip and inspire local churches and their prayer leaders in their desire to disciple their people in prayer and to become a "house of prayer for all nations." Its online store, prayershop.org, has more than 150 prayer resources available for purchase or download.

ISBN (Print): 978-1-935012-82-5
ISBN (E-Book): 978-1-935012-83-2

PrayerShop Publishing
P.O. Box 10667
Terre Haute, IN 47801

1 2 3 4 5 | 2022 2021 2020 2019 2018

Dedication

This book is dedicated to Annie, my wonderful wife of 38 years. She has partnered with me in life and ministry. Existence would be empty without her. Thank you, Sweet Bride.

Appreciation

I would be amiss not to thank my friend, Rene Roberts, who labored over this manuscript to make it all it can be.

I also want to express my love and appreciation for the team I worked alongside in Central's Prayer Ministry. What a team! They are outstanding leaders and became dear friends. In the beginning Rene Roberts relentlessly encouraged me to put a collection of thoughts and experiences of prayer in print. I also think of Cathy Cryer who has been my trusted associate for years. We have taken many prayer mountains together. Tony Vehon, Brittany Walker, Lisa Henry, Kurt Stromberg, Mike Fleming, Don Walker, Andy Moore, Brad Dalhman, Jerry Burke, Jim and Jo Butler, Ruth Graham, Rebecca Walker, Mark Merold, Sharon Bostic, Wanda Hall, and Ron Sciarro, who are all treasured friends and prayer leaders in their own right. Beyond these there are 50 or more who have encouraged me along the way and made our prayer ministries effective.

TABLE OF CONTENTS

This is a collection of prayer ideas that can be used personally, with a small group or in a larger prayer gathering. Many can be used in all three. We have included a key on the Table of Contents that alerts you for which prayer they are suited.

Personal Use = P
Small Group = SG
Larger Prayer Gathering = PG

INTRODUCTION

There are lots of reasons people struggle with prayer. One of those reasons is the lack of variety in their prayer life. Some people still use the same method of prayer they started using a decade or even multiple decades ago.

That is somewhat like a woman who keeps the same hairstyle for 20 or 30 years, or a friend of mine who went to the store and bought 10 pairs of black cotton cargo shorts and 15 blue t-shirts. He wears the same outfit each day.

In an effort to bring new life to the prayers of Christ followers over the last decade, I have started collecting creative ways to pray. *52 Creative Ways to Pray* is designed to give you new, time-tested methods of prayer to experiment with, in hopes that your personal or group prayer life will be refreshed. You can pick and choose, or try a new one each week for the next year. I hope that new excitement and life will stimulate your times with God, and His Kingdom will be enriched as a result.

Additional Note:

Many of these creative ways to pray can be used personally or in a small group. I have included some information on structuring prayer in groups with the hope it will be helpful.

If you are not leading prayer in a small group or larger prayer gathering, you can jump to Creative Way #1.

If you are a prayer leader, read the rest of the introduction for insights into freshening up prayer in your group.

Using Ideas in Small Groups or Group Prayer Gatherings
If you are a small group leader and desire to use some of these ideas to

expand or liven up the prayer times in your group, here are some suggestions and instructions.

I realize that, in most small groups, the prayer time is short, 10 to 15 minutes tops. (This is not true for those of you who lead prayer meetings.) My goal here is to provide practical and helpful information for whichever kind of meeting you have the chance to lead.

1. Prepare your heart.

The time of prayer in any gathering is a sacred trust. Effort is required not only in planning for the group meeting and the prayer time, but effort should also be taken to prepare your own heart.

Heart preparation may involve confession of known sin before the meeting or asking the Lord to use you for your group's wellbeing in a powerful way (see Creative Way #18).

2. Plan your meeting's prayer time.

As you seek the Lord's guidance for what prayer practice you should use in your prayer time, consider questions like these:

- Where is this meeting going?
- How can the prayer time unfold and interweave with the theme of the gathering?
- What do I want to see accomplished with our prayer time together?
- What methods of prayer will I use?
- Did I use any of these techniques last week?

As You Lead Prayer

Make it your goal that every member of your group gets comfortable with prayer. This is a non-negotiable objective for all your group members. Don't allow that person who never prays to stay in that place. Pray for individuals who struggle in this way; pray that each would begin to pray aloud and get comfortable doing so. Consider that goal as you select the ideas from this book.

Explain to the group the benefits of prayer and the power that rests there.

1. Help your members overcome self-consciousness when they begin to pray aloud.

I usually use and discuss a treasured video of my son, Ben, and grandson, Owen, "talking." My grandson was only one at the time and he does not say a single word that can be understood. My son asks, "What do you think, Owen?" Owen makes some sounds that are just precious but are not recognizable. Then Ben presses in more, "Is that right? Tell me more," he requests. Again, Owen makes some noises that are not distinguishable. I point out that my son does not scold Owen for not using sentences or correct grammar. He is thrilled that Owen is communicating at all.

Then we chat about the fact that this is the way God feels when we pray. He is not looking at sentence structure or for fancy words. He just wants to be in communication with us.

There is no such thing as "praying ugly!" Encourage your group members to get over their self-consciousness.

Satan is the one who tries to build the fear of prayer or concern of what others might think as we are praying. But these are not God's concerns in the slightest.

2. Share some of your prayers with the group so you can model praying for them.

Recently I was speaking at an event in Peoria, Illinois. My plane landed at O'Hare Airport at 4:19 p.m. and my flight to Peoria began boarding at 4:19 p.m. I was at the back of the plane . . . the very back . . . and my connecting gate was in another concourse. I sat in my seat thinking, *I may not make this connection. If I don't make that plane, I am fairly sure there is not another one today and I speak early tomorrow morning. If I don't make it, what will I do?*

My brain was on fire with swirling thought. In the midst of that, I determined to pray. "God I give this to You. I could stew on this and make myself sick or I can trust. I choose to trust." So I gave it to God in prayer. I did make it to the next concourse, with a minute or two to spare (no more)! But God got me through, again.

Sharing your prayer experiences is vital in helping others grow in their communication. Don't be afraid to do it and doing it often.

3. Help them to realize that the only person who does not want them to pray is Satan.

The devil will do anything to keep us from prayer because he knows how powerful prayer is. It is your job to expose his trickery and deception.

Consider Kinds of Prayer

A good prayer leader makes sure that people do not pray just for the same things each time. That is what this book is about—offering help in expanding the prayer lives of people and groups. You want to provide prayer times that try to give people an experience of prayer that is beyond the normal prayer they practice. So make sure that you rotate prayer ideas that touch on each of the basic kinds of prayer.

There are three basic kinds of prayer:
- Crisis Prayer – "Oh no, I have cancer."
- Casual Prayer – "I am late for the doctor's office. Please make all the lights between here and there be green."
- Kingdom Prayer – This type of prayer moves out of our needs and calls upon God to expand His Kingdom and rule on the earth.

Here are some examples of Kingdom prayers:
- Unity rather than competition in the churches where Christ is preached.
- That our greatest focus would be on reaching those who are not yet Christ followers.
- Halting the death of innocent babies' lives through abortion.
- Pray for God to call out His laborers into His harvest fields.
- Pray for the establishment of His Church and for His Kingdom here on earth to expand rapidly.
- Pray for the reputation of His name to be lifted up.
- Pray for barriers to the gospel to be removed.

Most prayer meetings are filled with casual prayers and that is not wrong. However, as the group progresses, we want them to pray more Kingdom-type prayers. It is not wrong to pray crises prayers either but most small groups and prayer groups would profit from praying more Kingdom prayers. We want to model Kingdom praying for our people and help them move in that direction.

Special Note for Leading Larger Prayer Gatherings

If you are a leader of larger prayer gatherings, I have found that having a participant or several participants pray for the pray-ers is extremely helpful. (I usually don't do this for a prayer time in a small group.) What do I mean by this?

While the prayer meeting is going on have someone or a few (if group is big enough) from the group go outside the location, but close by (another room off where the meeting is being held, a hallway, etc). Their task is to pray for those who are praying.

Have the person(s) pray the following kinds of objectives and other items for the pray-ers that God puts on their heart:
- for faith
- insight
- energy
- protection
- for the group to listen and hear from God.

If you want to include multiple people, you can rotate people out every seven to ten minutes during the prayer times to keep others involved.

At our church, I do a conference each year called Threshold Intensive (see p. 143). It is a four-day gathering where we discuss prayer, prayer leadership and prayer models that are working. It is not uncommon for us to have a team praying for each participant long before the event starts (months ahead of time). But this past year the goal was to create a team that would pray for the event and for those involved while the conference was going on in real time.

When I first heard of this practice frankly I thought it was a bit much. Then I attended a couple of gatherings where this was the practice and I was astounded at the difference it made. Don't write this off too quickly, like I did at first. We have found it to be powerful.

Use creativity

I believe the worst way to pray at your upcoming meeting is the way you prayed last week. This book is filled with practical and tested ways to pray. Use some of these methods in your prayer group or small group. I am convinced it will make your prayer times better.

Keep interest high.

Keeping the right balance between prayers, segments, and instructions moving and allowing for moments of silence and waiting on the Lord is a skill that is extremely valuable in leading prayer meetings. People—especially inexperienced pray-ers—can lose interest quickly if too much silent time occurs. It takes a while to learn, but sensitivity will come with time. Keep things moving in group prayer to make the prayer times more enjoyable.

There will be times when moments of silence are important, both because God speaks in them, and as a learning experience for your small or large group members. But most of the time, you will want to avoid long seasons of silence. It is more important to shut a dull prayer time down early than to let it be boring!

Let me show you what I did recently in a group prayer time, where the prayer practiced involved a lot of silence.

The theme was "forgiveness." The verse we used for the prayer time was John 8, the story of the woman caught in adultery. Jesus says in that passage, "Let any one of you who is without sin be the first to throw a stone at her" (1:7). I love that picture of people dropping stones of resentment and offense.

I began by asking people to reflect on those whom they have offended. Then, praying silently, we went through the exercise of asking God to forgive us for offending others we love. Instruction was also given to encourage group members not to leave their sin here, but to take the next step, which is to go to those they have offended and ask for their forgiveness (when and where appropriate).

Next, I moved them to consider those who have offended us. Again I called people to the place of forgiveness. I asked people to name silently in prayer those who have offended them and interchange the offense for forgiveness. I had given each person a stone as he or she entered the service that night. After a time of identifying those who had offended them, I asked them to kneel at the cross, which had been set up at the front of the church. They were instructed to pray, and then drop their stones of resentment, just as was done in Jesus' day.

Being creative, moving from one thing to another rapidly and using visuals can do wonders at keeping people engaged.

Have Fun

By being creative in small or large group prayer, you can work alongside the Holy Spirit to move people to deeper levels of prayer. This book is here to help you. I encourage you to let these ideas stimulate more in you!

– Paul Covert

CREATIVE WAY

Praying the Pictures

of Scripture

I enjoy praying the word pictures of Jesus in the Bible. All through the Gospels, there are vivid pictures of Jesus that are wonderful to pray. I am talking about the glimpses of Jesus' life that are so real that they create a picture in our minds.

For example, in Luke 9:37-43, Jesus comes down from the Mountain of Transfiguration and a great crowd gathers. A man, whose only son is harassed by a demon, cries out to Jesus, "Look upon my son." He goes on to say, "Your disciples tried to help but they were unable to." Jesus calls for the boy to be brought to him. On his way, the child is thrown on the ground by the unclean spirit. Jesus rebukes the demon and gives the child back to his father.

I love to pray with this picture in my mind when I pray for my sons (Annie and I have three grown sons). "Lord, look upon my sons and heal their struggles!" The image of Jesus giving the son back to his father is fabulous. Some people have a child who is estranged or ill. Praying the picture of Jesus giving their child back to them can be a powerful faith-builder for them.

Another example is that of Jesus feeding the 5,000 (John 6: 1-15).

I remember a day in ministry that was impossible. There were more needs for the day than were humanly possible to meet. I had a baby's fu-neral, a sermon to write, and 17 other things that needed attention. We have all had days like that.

That morning, I read of Jesus feeding the 5,000 and realized that He had more than enough resources to help me with my day if I would exert some faith. I prayed, "Lord, You are able to help me do and be all I need to do and be today." It turned out to be one of the most amazing days of my ministry in my 40 years of serving Him. God more than kept His part of the deal.

In Genesis chapter 15, there is this amazing passage where God puts Abram to sleep and He creates a covenant with Abram. In ancient times, usually when someone cut a covenant (that was the way it was described), each party had something to offer. You give me this much land and I will give you this much money.

In this case, however, Abram had nothing to give God, so God put Abram to sleep. Then the scripture says "When the sun had set and darkness had fallen, a smoking firepot with a blazing torch appeared and passed between the pieces" (Genesis 15:17). God realized that man could not keep his promise to Him, so God made a covenant with Himself.

From that picture, I would pray things like this: "Thank You, God, that You are in a covenant with me and I have all the benefits of that covenant. Thank You that You know and understand that I can't always keep my side of the bargain and You have already made allowances for that. I praise You that You always keep Your word. I rejoice in what this covenant means to me and entitles me to."

Obviously, there are thousands of pictures and many ways to pray each one. Give it a try. I think you will find it to be a blessing.

Practice

Here are a few Scripture pictures to get you started:
- Peter walking on the water (Matthew 14:22-33)
- God informing Moses that His name is I AM (Exodus 3:14)
- Jesus with the little children on His lap (Mark 10:13-16)
- Peter after denying Christ upon His death (Luke 22:54-62)

Small Group Tip

This idea can be used in a small group prayer time. The best way to use it is by planning ahead and selecting a specific need you will pray over that night, and the specific story from Scripture you will use.

When you begin, explain the method, present the need, then explain that as you read the scripture (or go around and have those in attendance read) that people should think of the need, and let what they visualize of the story guide what they pray.

You know you have it when . . .

Your mind's eye starts to visualize pictures of Jesus and God all through the Scriptures, and you can pray them freely. This will open up a new realm of prayer for you.

NOTES

_____

_____

_____

_____

_____

_____

_____

_____

CREATIVE WAY

Praying Your

Favorite Scriptures

Pick a favorite scripture. I recommend that you write it down (you could use the notes section at the end of this idea), but having your Bible open to it works, too.

Examine and think about the meaning of the verse carefully.

Next, pray the verse. First, thank God for what He has promised in the verse and then ask Him to do something in your life (or in the life of someone you are praying for) that the verse points to.

Practice

Let's use Acts 4:31 as an example. "After they prayed, the place where they were meeting was shaken. And they were all filled with the Holy Spirit and spoke the word of God boldly."

From this verse you could pray, "Lord Jesus, would You shake up my life with Your power and fill me with the Holy Spirit."

Or you could pray, "God help me to speak the word boldly."

How about praying, "God would You answer the prayer I have prayed and do so in the fashion that You did here in the book of Acts."

As you can see there are lots of ways to pray a favorite scripture. Just do it!

Here are some other great verses you can pray:

- Isaiah 26:3
- Philippians 4:6-7
- Psalm 23
- James 3:17
- Psalm 2:8
- Matthew 16:18

You know you have it when . . .

Your Bible study time starts to give you things to pray about. As you stay aware that you want to pray Scripture, it will fuel your prayer time.

In time, you will regularly find verses you will want to pray over your life and the lives of others. There is nothing like connecting your faith with God's promises and revelation of who He is.

Small Group Tip

When using this method in small groups—or in larger prayer gatherings—simply select a Scripture passage to use ahead of time. Look for something that talks of spiritual growth and biblical characteristic or fruit. They work very well in a public setting.

Here are two resources that can help you teach your group how to pray Scripture.

Solid Foundation: The Power of Praying Scripture is a little booklet that will motivate and equip people to pray God's Word back to Him. It is available at prayershop.org.

Fresh Prayer is a prayer meeting template that offers a passage of Scripture to pray and has questions to stimulate prayer from the passage. You can download it at waymakers.org. Click on "Pray" on the top toolbar, then click on "Fresh Prayer" on the left hand side of the page.

NOTES

_____

_____

_____

_____

_____

CREATIVE WAY

Praying the Riches

of Christ

The Scripture often points to the riches we have in Christ. But often what we have in Jesus Christ does not register with the average believer. Learning to appropriate these riches can happen through prayer!

This creative prayer method will show you how to pray that these riches would be activated in your life and the lives of those for whom you pray.

Practice

I love to collect these concepts of the riches of Christ and pray them over family or friends. I find it very powerful.

To show how to do this let's use Ephesians 1. The passage—using *The Message*—is below. (A hint: using *The Message* for any type of Scripture praying can bring a dynamic twist to prayer.) The riches given to us in this passage are underlined. If two are right next to each other, the second one is italicized so you will notice both of the riches.

Read the passage and then pray these riches over yourself or someone you care about.

Verses 1-2: I, Paul, am under God's plan as an apostle, a special agent of Christ Jesus, writing to you faithful believers in Ephesus. I greet you with the <u>grace and peace poured into our lives by God</u> our Father and our Master, Jesus Christ.

Verse 3-6: How blessed is God! And what a blessing he is! He's the Father of our Master, Jesus Christ, <u>and takes us to the high places of blessing in him</u>. Long before he laid down earth's foundations, he had us in mind, had <u>settled on us as the focus of his love</u>, <u>*to be made whole and holy by his love*</u>. Long, long ago he decided to adopt us into his family through Jesus Christ. (What pleasure he took in planning this!) <u>He wanted us to enter into the celebration of his lavish gift-giving by the hand of his beloved Son.</u>

Verses 7-10: Because of the sacrifice of the Messiah, his blood poured out on the altar of the Cross, we're a free people—free of penalties and punishments chalked up by all our misdeeds. And not just barely free, either. *Abundantly* <u>free!</u> He thought of everything, <u>provided for everything we could possibly need,</u> letting us in on the plans he took such delight in making. He set it all out before us in Christ, a long-range plan in which everything would be brought together and summed up in him, everything in deepest heaven, everything on planet earth.

Verses 11-14: <u>It's in Christ that we find out who we are and what we are living for.</u> Long before we first heard of Christ and got our hopes up, he had his eye on us, <u>had designs on us for glorious living</u>, part of the overall purpose he is working out in everything and everyone. It's in Christ that you, once you heard the truth and believed it (this message of your salvation), found yourselves home free—signed, sealed, and delivered by the Holy Spirit. This signet from God is the first installment on what's coming, a reminder that we'll get everything God has planned for us, a praising and glorious life.

Verses 15-19: That's why, when I heard of the solid trust you have in the Master Jesus and your outpouring of love to all the followers of Jesus, I couldn't stop thanking God for you—every time I prayed, I'd think of you and give thanks. But I do more than thank. I ask—ask the God of our Master, Jesus Christ, the God of glory—to make you intelligent and discerning in knowing him personally, your eyes focused and clear, so that you can see exactly what it is he is calling you to do, <u>grasp the immensity of this glorious way of life he has</u> <u>for his followers,</u> oh, the utter extravagance of his work in us who trust him—<u>endless energy, boundless strength</u>!

Verses 20-23: All this energy issues from Christ: God raised him from death and set him on a throne in deep heaven, in charge of running the universe, everything from galaxies to governments, <u>no name</u> <u>and no power exempt from his rule</u>. And not just for the time being, but <u>*forever.*</u> He is in charge of it all, <u>has the final word on every-</u> <u>thing</u>. At the center of all this, Christ rules the church. The church, you see, is not peripheral to the world; the world is peripheral to the church. The church is Christ's body, in which he speaks and acts, by which he fills everything with his presence.

Take some time to digest the riches of Christ in this text.

After you have noted the riches of Christ, select several friends or loved ones you want to pray those blessings over. Maybe even send them a note and let them know what you prayed over them today.

You will know when you have it when . . .

You begin regularly to think of praying these riches over yourself and your friends.

NOTES

_____

_____

_____

_____

_____

_____

_____

_____

CREATIVE WAY

"Standing Firm"

Prayer

When was the last time you took a stand for something in prayer? It may have been awhile. That is going to change this week. We are going to take a stand for a different issue each day.

Practice

We have a tendency to be soft in our lives and forget to stand up for things that are worthy of a good fight. This happens with biblical truths, too. The biblical call to stand firm is very clear. This command is found numerous times in the both the Old and New Testaments.

"Be on your guard; **stand firm** in the faith; be courageous; be strong. Do everything in love" (1 Corinthians 16:13-14).

"Therefore, my dear brothers and sisters**, stand firm**. Let nothing move you. Always give yourselves fully to the work of the Lord, because you know that your labor in the Lord is not in vain" (1 Corinthians 15:58).

"Standing Firm" Prayer is where you simply select a biblical truth and pray that into your life or the life of someone you love.

To practice, pick seven items you are willing to stand firm for in prayer and write them in the notes section below. Then each day, stand firm for one of those concerns.

Here are a few to get you started.

I am willing to stand for the Name of God and His reputation.
Daniel did this when he was told not to pray any longer. He took a stand for God and continued to pray three times a day (Daniel 6:10).

I am willing to stand on the promises He has made to us.
Because Daniel stood for the name of God, it got him thrown in the lion's den. That was the perfect opportunity for Daniel to cave in and stop standing, but he didn't. He chose to stand on the promises of God, which resulted in his safety even in an actual lions' den.

I am willing to stand on the truth of who God says I am and not what others might think or say.

I am a child of God	I am a joint heir with Jesus
I am chosen by God	I am adopted by God
I am loved by God	I am set apart for God and His service

I am willing to stand on the truth of His protection for me and my family.
"'No weapon forged against you will prevail, and you will refute every tongue that accuses you. This is the heritage of the servants of the LORD, and this is their vindication from me,' says the LORD." (Isaiah 54:17)

I am willing to stand on the truth of His provision for me.
"Therefore I tell you, do not worry about your life, what you will eat or drink; or about your body, what you will wear. Is not life more than food, and the body more than clothes? Look at the birds of the air; they do not sow or reap or store away in barns, and yet your heavenly Father feeds them. Are you not much more valuable than they? Can any one of you by worrying add a single hour to your life?

"And why do you worry about clothes? See how the flowers of the field grow. They do not labor or spin. Yet I tell you that not even Solomon in all his splendor was dressed like one of these. If that is how God clothes the grass of the field, which is here today and tomorrow is thrown into the fire, will he not much more clothe you—you of little faith? So do not worry, saying, 'What shall we eat?' or 'What shall we drink?' or 'What shall we wear?' For the pagans run after all these things, and your heavenly Father knows that you need them. But seek first his kingdom and his righteousness, and all these things will be given to you as well." (Matthew 6: 25-33)

I am willing to stand on His plan for my future.
"Do not let your hearts be troubled. You believe in God; believe also in me. My Father's house has many rooms; if that were not so, would I have told you that I am going to prepare a place for you?" (John 14:1-2)

Now you try. Take some time to think about the things you are willing to fight for and stand firm. After you have compiled a list, pray over each one and ask for the courage to stand firm in that area.

You know you have it when . . .
You find yourself standing firm over matters often and this type of praying is included in your regular arsenal of prayer.

NOTES

_____

_____

_____

_____

_____

_____

_____

_____

CREATIVE WAY

The "Thank You"

Walk

I live in a neighborhood that takes about 30 minutes to walk around it at a pleasant pace. This has led me to a way to pray that has lifted my spirits many times. I call it the "Thank You" Walk.

As soon as I open the front door for my walk, I just start thanking God for everything I can think of. That is all I do on the walk. No matter what mood I am in when I start, I am always on a mountain top when I return.

You just can't spend time thanking God and not have your spirit lifted. Annie, my wife, and I like to do this together when we can.

"Enter his gates with thanksgiving and his courts with praise; give thanks to him and praise his name" (Psalm 100:4).

". . . speaking to one with psalms, hymns, and songs from the Spirit. Sing and make music from your heart to the Lord, always giving thanks to God the Father for everything, in the name of our Lord Jesus Christ" (Ephesians 5:19-21).

At least three times this week go for a "Thank You" Walk. It is ok to take a friend or spouse, just get out there and go! You will be amazed at what it does for your attitude.

You know you have it when . . .

You start to become thankful the minute you walk out of the house!

A friend of mine is the most grateful man I know. You can't be around him for any length of time and not hear his expressions of gratitude. After I am around some people for a while, I am ready to be by myself or with new friends. Not this guy. I count the days until I get to be around him again because his appreciativeness is so infectious. He influences me so heavily that after I am with him, my wife can tell. She will say, "You have been hanging out with Mike (not his real name) again, haven't you?" When I leave his presence I am energized, renewed, and refreshed.

Learn to be grateful and life will be better.

NOTES

_____

_____

_____

_____

_____

_____

_____

_____

CREATIVE WAY

Blessing

Others

Blessing is the act of communicating approval or encouragement to others we care about. Blessing is a powerful concept in the Scriptures. God blessed Adam and Eve when He created them and placed them in the garden. Before he died, Jacob had a blessing for each of his twelve sons, recorded in Genesis 49.

Here is Isaac's blessing for his son, Jacob, from Genesis 27:27-29:
So he went to him and kissed him. When Isaac caught the smell of his clothes, he blessed him and said, "Ah, the smell of my son is like the smell of a field that the LORD has blessed. May God give you heaven's dew and earth's richness—an abundance of grain and new wine. May nations serve you and peoples bow down to you. Be lord over your brothers, and may the sons of your mother bow down to you. May those who curse you be cursed and those who bless you be blessed."

One of the joys of my life is gathering my grandchildren on my lap and praying a prayer of blessing over each of them. I pray for:
- their safety;

- their walk with God;
- their future spouses;
- strong health;
- sensitivity to the Spirit of God;
- love for their siblings;
- for favor with God and man;
- and on and on.

Then I give them each a kiss and a huge hug, and send them home with their parents. This has become a family tradition and a happy time for all of us.

The concept is transferable. You could biblically pray a blessing over your husband or wife before they leave for work in the morning. You could pray a blessing over your children at night before bed. Praying a blessing over your neighbors or even your enemies would be a healthy and spiritually wonderful thing to do.

Small Group Tip

You could have a night where you just pray blessings over each other. Provide some from Scripture for people to use if they cannot come up with blessings of their own.

Practice

This week, look for someone you can bless each day. It might be a family member or friend. Select a different one for each day.

Go to them (ask their permission to demonstrate this blessing). Look for a private spot where they will not be embarrassed, place a hand on them (if that is appropriate) and pray a blessing over them. Pray over their health, their future, their relationships, their walk with God and so on.

You know you have it when . . .

Blessing others is just part of your normal daily routine. Imagine how many people would be refreshed and strengthen by your prayers in this way.

NOTES

_____

_____

_____

_____

_____

_____

_____

_____

CREATIVE WAY

Community

of Prayer

We have found value in connecting a group of friends or a community in prayer over particularly tough prayer needs.

My wife prayed for her mom to come to faith for 45 years. I prayed for her mom for 35 years (since I joined the family after she had already begun the prayer). The truth is we saw no external movement from those prayers. Her positions did not change; her attitude toward God was mostly the same. There was no noticeable progress.

Remember when Aaron and Hur held up Moses' arms as Israel battled the Amalekites in Exodus 17? As long as Moses' arms were raised, the Israelites prevailed in battle. But, when his arms dropped, the Amalekites began to be victorious. Through the years, we have recruited a team of 12 intercessors who pray for us as well as our ministry—they hold up our arms, if you will. We also pray for them. They are dear and trusted friends we can share our greatest struggles with.

Since little progress was visible with this answer to prayer for Annie's mom, we came up with an idea to invite a community of friends to join us in praying for Jackie (Annie's mom) on a certain day. We let them all know several weeks in advance, and then we prayed on that day. Still, we saw no movement. We waited six months and asked them to pray again. This time, within a week, she had received Christ . . . after 45 years of prayer.

I believe this is a good method for those prayer needs that don't seem to be moving and no visible progress can be detected. Find some trusted friends and invite them in to join you in prayer on a specific day.

Practice

Give some thought to some of those very "hard ground" kinds of prayers you are praying. List them below and then connect with at least five others for a day of prayer and fasting (or just prayer) over one of those needs. It may take more than one day of prayer on each topic but we have seen fruit with this type of community praying.

NOTES

_____

_____

_____

_____

_____

_____

_____

_____

_____

CREATIVE WAY

Life

Prayer

Many believers have a life verse. Mine is 2 Corinthians 5:9 "So we make it our goal to please him, whether we are at home in the body or away from it." This goal makes life simple. No matter what the situation, my goal needs to be to please Christ.

If you have a life verse, why not have a life prayer? The desire and content of such a prayer becomes something that you pray over and over. You meditate on it and pray it regularly.

This prayer bubbles up from the depths of your soul. Life prayers are Kingdom-centered prayers, not something personal like, "Give me a new car." Life prayers find their source in our deepest feelings and emotions.

My life prayer is for the American Church to invest more in prayer. We have gotten lazy about depending on God in prayer here in the States. We have so few needs that are beyond our capability of doing something about here in this country, that we somehow begin to think we can do it alone, without God's help. I long to see America and the American Church more engaged in prayer.

How about you? Is there a prayer that God is calling you to pray? If so, why not make it your life prayer, and pray it often.

Maybe the best way to illustrate the concept of a life prayer is to introduce you to a woman I ran into in Albania one spring on a prayer journey. Suzanna and her husband, Jack, a pastor, had lived in Virginia when they took on the challenge to pray more strategically for the world. They began to pray for Albania, during the time when Albania was one of the most anti-Christian places in the entire world.

As they prayed one day, God moved Suzanna to go to the store to buy black and white striped "prison cloth" to make curtains for her dining room. She hesitated at first and had a lot of excuses. "God that will not match what we have in the room." "God, no one carries 'prison cloth.' I could look for years before I'm able to find it."

But the Lord did not let up on Suzanna, and she finally went in search of the fabric that God had instructed her to buy. Not so incredibly—God knows what He's doing—the first store had enough "prison cloth" for her to make curtains for all of the dining room windows! So she made the curtains.

Because Suzanna had a heart for those Albanians imprisoned because of their faith, she felt she should keep the curtains drawn. When she heard of a Christian being released from prison in Albania, she would open the curtains for three days, but then close them again to remind her to pray. Suzanna and Jack have nine children, and her curtains attracted quite a bit of attention with all the people and activity in their home. This gave her the opportunity to share her story of prayer for Albania over and over again.

When Albania fell from communism in 1991, Suzanna and Jack were some of the first workers to move there to begin mission work. Now she and Jack are more than 80 years old and have been praying and serving for many, many years!

I stood with Suzanna in a trash dump in Albania singing songs about Jesus with a group of gypsy children. It was incredibly moving to witness Suzanna's life prayer fulfilled before my eyes.

Is God calling you to pray for something for the good of His Kingdom? Why not start today?

Practice

Life prayers are more than simple requests. They are asking God for big things in His Kingdom. Things like:

- The end of human trafficking in our world.
- For North Korea to stop the persecution of Christians and come to faith.
- For the end of sexual corruption and perversion in our nation.
- The end of racial tensions and strife.

Take some time and pray this week to think about a worthy life prayer you could embrace. This may require several days of prayer or even a month. Continue to seek God about your life prayer until He puts something on your heart. Then write it below and begin to pray.

You know you have it when . . .

God gives you a life verse and you begin to pray over it semi-regularly.

NOTES

_____

_____

_____

_____

_____

_____

_____

_____

CREATIVE WAY

Praying the Characters and
Characteristics of a Scripture Passage

Y ou can learn a lot from looking closely at the characters in a Bible passage. Studying them can give you lots of exciting ways to pray.

Practice

Take a passage of Scripture and examine it for the characters in the text and how they are portrayed. For example, in Psalm 86, we see a requester (which is us) and God. I have prepared some thoughts for you from this chapter to get you started in this method of prayer.

Requests from the requester
> V1 - Hear, O Lord
> V1 - Answer me
> V2 - Guard my life
> V2 - Save your servant
> V4 - Bring joy to your servant
> V6 - Hear my prayer
> V6 - Listen to my cry for mercy
> V11 - Teach me your ways and I will walk in truth

V11 - Give me an undivided heart that I may fear your name

V16 - Turn to me and have mercy on me

V16 - Grant your strength to your servant

V16 - Save the son of your maidservant

V17 - Give me a sign of your goodness

Description of the Requester

V1 - poor and needy

V2 - I am devoted to you

V2 - You are my God

V2 - Trusts in you

V3 - Have mercy on me

V3 - I call on you all day long

V4 - For to you, oh Lord, I life up my soul

V7 - In the day of trouble I will call to you

V12 - I will praise you with all my heart

V12 - I will glorify your name forever

V14 - The arrogant are attacking me

V14 - A band of ruthless men seek my life

V17 - For you Lord have helped me and comforted me

Descriptions of God

V5 - You are forgiving and good

V5 - Abounding in love to all who call on you

V7 - You will answer me

V8 - Among the gods, there is none like you

V8 - No deeds can compare with yours

V9 - All the nations you have made will come and worship before you

V9 - They will bring glory to your name

V10 - You are great and do marvelous deeds

V10 - You alone are God

V13 - Great is your love toward me

V13 - You have delivered me from the depths of the grave

V15 - But you are a compassionate and generous God

V15 - Slow to anger, abounding in love and faithfulness

Another wonderful passage to study the characters is Luke 11:5-13

In this passage, we have several characters:

- The guest who shows up and needs food
- The host who is obligated to provide for the guest
- The rich man who has bread

Notice the dilemma the host is in. He is obligated to go ask the rich man for food late at night. This was not convenient and could result in repercussions.

Then take note of how we are portrayed in the passage. We are the hosts who are asked to bring guests' (even strangers) needs to God by prayer.

How God is pictured? Not like the crabby rich man who does not want to help. This is the opposite of our God's response to prayer.

The idea with a passage is to take what you have gleaned from the text and use those elements in prayer. Pray through a passage of Scripture, but rather than simply praying verses back to God, use what you discern from the passage to guide your prayers.

You will now you have it when . . .

Learning to pray about the wonderful characters and characteristics you read about in Scripture becomes fertile soil for prayer.

NOTES

_____

_____

_____

_____

_____

_____

_____

_____

CREATIVE WAY

Praying a

Song

Song can spur us to prayer very effectively. Songs like "It Is Well with My Soul" or many contemporary songs are wonderful springboards for us to pray. I love using Rend Collective's song "More than Conquerors." But there are hundreds you could use!

Practice

This can be done as a personal prayer practice, but it works well in group prayer as well.

1. Pick a worship/intercession song or hymn.
2. Download the song from iTunes, YouTube, etc., and bring it on your phone or tablet.
3. Print off the lyrics. If in a group, print one sheet per person. At the beginning of the meeting, explain what you're going to do and how you will use the worship song to fuel the intercession.
4. Play the song once, with each person listening and worshiping.
5. Depending on the size of the group, you can all stay together or you can break into groups of 3-4 for prayer. The first time you do it, you

may want to stay in one group until everyone understands what you are doing. I actually prefer to pray all together allowing prayers to be spontaneous. That way people who are not comfortable are not put on the spot.

6. Take time to look over the first verse and encourage each person to pick a word, phrase or entire line that jumps out to him or her.

7. If in groups, go around the circle, have each person take a turn, saying his or her phrase/sentence and then praying a sentiment that the word/phrase stimulates in them. (Note it is ok for people to pass if they are not yet comfortable. I allow this in all my group prayer sessions.) If you are in one large group, allow anyone to pray at any time, but stay targeted on a specific verse of the song. Move on when you feel you should move on.

8. Next, do the same with the second verse, going around the circle giving each person a chance to share and pray.

9. If time and the song allows, do more rounds praying through whatever verses, chorus and bridge the song has.

10. Finally play the song again, everyone singing, worshiping, praying – in whatever style they feel led. Then end with "free for all prayers," basically anything left over on someone's heart.

Some group-prayer reminders:

Determine ahead of time how long you will give the group to pray through each verse and make it clear to them. So for instance, if you have an hour slot for prayer, and you need 5:22 for the song at the beginning and end, plus time for explanation, then you have 3 rounds of prayer at roughly 10 plus minutes each, etc.

If you are breaking into smaller groups, encourage them to keep going around the circle multiple times praying rather than wait for other groups to finish. No need to chat or be silent waiting for what's next.

Remember, don't get stuck on the form or be 100% tied to the structure of it. If the prayers seem highlighted in a unique and powerful way, linger. Don't move on. This exercise is just to get prayer juices flowing. Allow room for Holy Spirit to inspire prayers and lead you in to intercession for whatever place/topic, etc., He has shown you.

NOTES

_____

_____

_____

_____

_____

_____

_____

_____

_____

CREATIVE WAY

Sentence

Prayers

Many people are reluctant to pray out loud in a group. They can be worried about how their prayers will sound to others or they simply lack the confidence to vocalize their prayers. To help them overcome this fear, we teach praying sentence prayers. These are already-constructed sentences and all that is required is to fill in the blank.

As a leader, you just ask people to pray and fill in the blank. Put the sentence on a screen or print it out and explain how it will be used in group prayer.

For example: "God I worship you because you are _____
_____."

Sentence prayers are a great way to encourage people to pray out loud in a fairly non-threatening way. Once your group has mastered sentence praying, it is usually not long until they are taking new strides in prayer.

Practice

Here are several sentence prayers you can use. Note: It is a great idea to give reluctant pray-ers a list of these sentence prayers. Encourage them to pray them out loud even when they are alone. This will help them grow accustom to the sound of their voice praying.

Thank You God for _____.
Please help me to encourage _____ today.
God, I need Your wisdom today in _____
(name a situation for which you need God's wisdom).
Father please give me peace in the situation with _____
_____ today. (Name an area of your life where you need God's peace.)

Use in Personal Prayer

I confess, God, I struggle with _____;
please help me.
Help me to forgive _____ like You have forgiven me.

A Variation of Sentence Prayers

You can also do sentence prayers that focus on one topic.

They would look like this: "Father, we pray that you would draw our nation to _____." The blank might get filled in with peace; unity, repentance, or humility. These prayers could be prayed individually or as a group. Either way, the prayers would focus on this one topic for the nation or whatever topic you choose.

When praying in a group, prayer when it is done well is like a diamond that shimmers from multiple facets. Each person brings different thoughts and feelings to the prayer time that result in richness in prayer. This kind of praying gives cohesion to the prayer time and covers the need from several perspectives.

You know you have it when . . .

Your group can stay on one subject and not wander off. This takes practice but creates fabulous prayer times and connection.

Practice

Consider praying one of these focused prayers each day this week either in your small group or individually.

- The Church
- The lost
- The hurting
- The governmental leaders
- The end of social injustice
- The nations that do not know Christ
- For persecuted believers around the world

NOTES

_____

_____

_____

_____

_____

_____

_____

_____

CREATIVE WAY

Praying the

Promises

Another tremendous way to pray is to repeat back to God the promises He has made to us.

In June of 2016, I started having trouble seeing. It was awful. My vision deteriorated to the point I could not see the big "E" at the optometrist's office, at least for a while. Obviously, I was scared and anxious.

Because I was not seeing well, instead of reading my Bible, I started listening to the word daily. I found myself listening to Epistles of the Bible 40 or 50 times in a row. I used several translations as I bathed in the Word.

One day as I was listening to the book of Philippians from the Message, my ears picked up when I heard chapter 3:15-16. It was as if God was speaking directly to me in these verses. I ran the audio back several times and began to claim the meaning in my life instantly.

"So let's keep focused on that goal, those of us who want everything God has for us. If any of you have something else in mind, something less than total commitment, God will clear your blurred vision—you'll see it yet! Now that we're on the right track, let's stay on it."

Even though these verses are focused on total commitment, I felt like God was communicating with me and lovingly reassuring me that He was going to clear up my blurred vision. I found myself reminding God of this promise almost daily. You cannot imagine the comfort that has come in the midst of the struggle from standing on this pledge and appealing to God on the basis of this pledge.

In brief, God was faithful to His Word. He protected me from misdiagnosis and a hasty treatment plan that would have destroyed by optic nerves. Several months later it was determined that I had Crion's disease, which stands for chronic reoccurring inflammation of the optic nerve. It is a rare disease. We don't know what causes it but it can be controlled by medication. So as I write this I am stable and still believe that I will be healed, because I continue to hold the position of faith and the promise from God.

Practice

Below you will find some of God's promises. Pick out a different promise and pray it each day. Or have a time in your small group when you pray these promises over each other.

Prayer
- Before they call, I will answer (Isaiah 65:24)
- Delight in the Lord, He gives the desires of your heart (Psalm 37:4)
- Commit your way to Lord, He will bring it to pass (Psalm 37:5)
- Call on me and I will show you great and mighty things (Jeremiah 33:3)
- You have made heaven . . . nothing is too hard for You (Jeremiah 32:17-18)
- If any two agree . . . ask, it will be done (Matthew 18:19)

Peace
- Keep you in perfect peace (Isaiah 26:3)
- Work of righteousness will be peace (Isaiah 32:17)
- The thoughts I think toward you are peace, not evil (Jeremiah 29:11)
- The end of the upright man is peace (Psalm 37:37)

Protection
- He shall deliver from snare, pestilence, terror, arrow (Psalm 91:3)
- No weapon formed against you will prosper (Isaiah 54:17)

- When you pass through water, it will not overflow you (Isaiah 43:2)
- I will make you a bronze wall, they will not prevail (Jeremiah 15:20)
- Those who trust You, shout for joy, You defend them (Psalm 5:11-12)

Supply
- Lions do hunger . . . but you shall not lack any good thing (Psalm 34:10)
- I have not seen the righteous forsaken or begging (Psalm 37:25)
- My God shall supply all your need (Philippians 4:19)
- God is able to make all grace abound to you (2 Corinthians 9:8)

Success
- Then He shall make your way prosperous, and have success (Joshua 1:8)
- Whatsoever he does, it shall prosper (Psalm 1:3)
- All things work together for good to him who loves God (Romans 8:28)

Strength
- He gives strength to the weary (Isaiah 40:29)
- They that wait on the Lord renew their strength (Isaiah 40:31)
- Fear not for I am with you . . . I will help you (Isaiah 41:10)
- The Lord will hold your right hand (Isaiah 41:13)
- My grace is sufficient for you (2 Corinthians 12:9)

Deliverance
- The righteous cry and the Lord hears and delivers them from trouble (Psalm 34:17)
- The angel of the Lord encamps around those who fear Him (Psalm 34:7)
- When the enemy comes like a flood . . . the Lord will stand against him (Isaiah 59:19)

Direction and Leading
- In all your ways acknowledge Him and He will direct your paths (Proverbs 3:6)
- You will hear a voice behind you saying, "This is the way, walk in it" (Isaiah 30:21)

- Commit your way to the Lord . . . and your plans will be established (Proverbs 16:3,9)
- A good man's steps are ordered by the Lord (Psalm 37:23)
- The Lord will guide you always (Isaiah 58:11)
- I will instruct and teach you the way to go (Psalm 32:8)

Fears
- God gave not the spirit of fear, but of sound mind (2 Timothy 1:7)
- Fear not for I am with you, I will help you (Isaiah 41:6,10,13)
- I sought Him and He delivered me from all my fears (Psalm 34:4)

Souls
- Ask of me and I will make the nations your inheritance (Psalm 2:8)
- He who sows and weeps . . . will return with joy, carrying sheaves with him (Psalm 126:6)
- Lord is not slow . . . He's not willing any should perish (2 Peter 3:9)

Your Children
- All your children will be taught of the Lord (Isaiah 54:13)
- Children are a heritage of the Lord . . . your reward (Psalm 127:3)
- My words will not depart out of your descendant's mouth (Isaiah 59:21)
- I will pour out My Spirit on your offspring (Isaiah 44:3)
- Train up a child . . . when old . . . he will not depart from it (Proverbs 22:6)

Wisdom
- Lord gives me tongue of the learned to know how to speak (Isaiah 50:4)
- The law . . . is perfect . . . making wise the simple (Psalm 19:7)
- Fear of the Lord is beginning of knowledge (Proverbs 1:7)
- Lack wisdom? Ask God, who gives generously to all men (James 1:5)

Forgiveness
- You, Lord, are forgiving . . . abounding in love (Psalm 86:5)
- If we confess our sins, He is faithful . . . to forgive (1 John 1:9)

- Though your sins be as scarlet they shall be white as snow (Isaiah 1:18)
- I am He Who blots out transgressions (Isaiah 43:25)

Ability above Impossibility
- Lord God . . . there is nothing too hard for You (Jeremiah 32:17,27)
- He who began a good work in you will perform it (Philippians 1:6)
- The word of His grace . . . is able to build you up (Acts 20:32)
- He is able to do exceedingly abundantly . . . by His power at work in us (Ephesians 3:20)
- He is able to keep you . . . present you faultless (Jude 24)

Healing
- I am the Lord who heals you (Exodus 15:26)
- Who forgives all . . . and heals all your diseases (Psalm 103:3)
- The prayer of faith shall make the sick person well (James 5:15)
- He took our infirmities and carried our diseases (Matthew 8:17)

Sleep
- You will lie down and your sleep will be sweet (Proverbs 3:24)
- I will . . . sleep, for You make me dwell in safety (Psalm 4:8)
- He grants sleep to those He loves (Psalm 127:2)

Word of God
- Shall not return void . . . shall accomplish and prosper (Isaiah 55:11)
- Is like a fire . . . like a hammer (Jeremiah 23:29)
- Is able to build you up and give you inheritance (Acts 20:32)
- Is quick, powerful, sharp, piercing, dividing, discerning (Hebrews 4:12)
- Is not bound (2 Timothy 2:9)
- Is profitable for doctrine, reproof, instruction (2 Timothy 3:16)

You know you have it when . . .

You believe what you are praying. Mastery of this type is prayer is not just finding the promises and praying them back, but learning to lean on them and trust in the midst of major adversities.

NOTES

CREATIVE WAY

Praying Scripturally

for Good Government

One of the best things we can pray for is our nation and government. In fact, 1 Timothy 2:1-4 challenges us to pray for all those in authority.

Sometimes I get discouraged praying for our nation because I see so little improvement in our leaders and their policies after I pray. But prayer can turn the tide in our nation. Carol Ann Hale Kononova has discovered an outstanding way to pray for our nation. In her guide "A Scriptural Prayer for Good Government," Kononova has listed 33 scriptural prayers to pray.

Practice

You could use this guide in your small group prayer time or a larger prayer gathering. Simply provide a copy to everyone or put it on a screen and pray through it.

For personal use, I have broken this into Scriptures each day to pray over our government.

Monday
- Heavenly Father, I give thanks for our government and its leaders. (1 Tim. 2:1)

- I pray for all men and women having governmental authority over us. (1 Tim. 2:2)
- Pour out YOUR Spirit upon them and make YOUR Word known to them. (Prov. 1:23)
- Help them to be men and women of integrity with an understanding of YOUR principles, acting justly and righteously. (Ps. 25:21)

Tuesday

- May we lead a quiet and peaceable life, in all godliness and honesty. (1 Tim. 2:2)
- Give our leaders wise and understanding hearts, and let godly knowledge be pleasant to them. (Prov. 2:10)
- Guide them in making wise and godly choices; guard over them with understanding, keeping them out of danger. (Prov. 2:11)
- Deliver them from the way of evil and from evil men. (Prov. 2:12)

Wednesday

- Make their hearts and ears attentive to godly counsel. (Psalm 1:1)
- Empower them to do what is right in YOUR sight. (2 Chron. 20:32)
- Give us upright, just and fair men and women in our government, that our nation would be secure. (Isa. 54:14)
- Sustain those who live right and blameless before YOU and keep them firm and strong. (Prov. 2:21)

Thursday

- Shake all areas harboring corruption and ungodliness in our land. (Heb. 12:27)
- Cut off the wicked. Let the unfaithful be rooted out. (Prov. 2:22)
- Bring to light the hidden things done in darkness, and expose the secret dishonesty of their hearts. (1 Cor. 4:5)
- Cause this nation to remember from where we have fallen, repenting, and returning to righteous and godly works. (Rev. 2:5)

Friday

- Humbling ourselves, praying, and turning from our wicked ways. We acknowledge that then YOU will hear us, O Lord, and forgive our sins and heal our land. (2 Chron. 7:14)
- Open our eyes and turn us, as a nation, from darkness to light. (Acts 26:18)
- Soften our hearts, for we recognize we are hardened through the deceitfulness of sin. (Heb. 3:13)
- Send YOUR Word once again to the people of our nation and rescue us from destructions (Ps. 107:20)
- Father, thank YOU that YOU have been longsuffering toward us, not willing that any should perish, but that all should come to repentance. (2 Peter 3:9)

Saturday

- Raise up a standard of godliness and righteousness in our nation. (Isa. 49:22)
- Bring the rains of YOUR Spirit to flood this land and awaken us once again. (Zech. 10:1)
- Revive YOUR work in the midst of us. (Hab. 3:2)
- Raise up intercessors and those who will stand watch over our nation (Isa. 59:16)

Sunday

- Give us discernment and understanding to pull down strongholds over our land. (2 Cor. 10:4)
- Let the glory of the Lord be revealed! (Isa. 40:5)
- Arise, shine through YOUR people and fill our land with YOUR light and truth. (Isa. 60:1-4)
- Set our hearts and our souls to seek first YOU, Lord, and YOUR righteousness. (1 Chron. 22:19)

Praying for the government should not be a strain or cumbersome for believers. This prayer is a start in that direction. But always look for more powerful ways to pray for our nation and its leaders.

You know you have it when . . .

Praying for government becomes a natural and regular part of your or your group's prayer time.

NOTES

_____

_____

_____

_____

_____

_____

_____

_____

Adapted from "A Scriptural Prayer for Good Government" by Carol Ann Hale Kononova. Used with permission.

CREATIVE WAY

Praying the Jackson Style

Several years ago, we had a pastor from Uganda visit our church and he taught us to pray all at the same time, out loud. It was the first time we had tried this method and it was a big hit. His name was Jackson Senyonga so this style of prayer became known by us as "Jackson style."

Most people know it as "Korean Style" since that is how Korean churches pray together. But actually, many Asian and African churches pray this way.

This is a wonderful way to teach prayer to those who are new at it. I had a new pray-er in the prayer room recently and his comment was, "Praying makes me nervous because I pray ugly." New pray-ers who are exposed to "Jackson style" prayer get used to hearing their voices praying along with many others. This method takes away the, "How does my voice or prayer sound when I pray with others?" It silences the demons of, "My prayers don't sound as good as so and so's," because they realize no one is really listening to their prayer . . . except God.

I think praying in this fashion is better for new pray-ers than the traditional method where just one person prays and the others listen and agree. It certainly takes away the pressure that can be present. "Jackson style" prayer does require some extra concentration because you do hear what others are praying at first. The upside of hearing others' prayers is they remind me of things I also want to pray about.

Practice

In your next prayer time or corporate prayer meeting, experiment with "Jackson Style" prayer.

I usually set it up by asking people to say their address out loud all at the same time. Then I say, "On three: ready, one, two, three, go," and they begin. Then I say, "That was good but it needs to be a little louder." This time say your phone number out loud on the count of three. They pray louder this time and that is usually about the right level. Then I say. "OK, that was good! So let's begin to pray now all together out loud. Ready, begin."

It will take several times for your people to get comfortable with this. So be prepared to do "Jackson Style" prayer once a month until people master this style.

We have found it helpful to do it for a set time as well. The leader would say, "We are going to pray for our city, Jackson Style, for the next three minutes." That way people have some idea how long we will be using this method.

We use "Jackson Style" prayer in our service intercession prayer rooms when we have more prayer requests than can humanly be covered in an hour. We will pray one person at a time until the time is almost gone and then we move to "Jackson Style" for the remaining material. This allows us to cover all the requests and make sure each one gets prayed over.

You know you have it when . . .

Your group becomes comfortable praying this way and even begins to enjoy it. You will also know it when your times of praying this way get longer and multiple prayers stay strong.

NOTES

_____

_____

_____

_____

_____

_____

CREATIVE WAY

"Who I Am in

Christ" Prayer

One of Satan's favorite tactics is to use someone or something to give us a name that is not true about ourselves.

I was traveling with a team in Malaysia on a prayer journey a few years ago. I noticed one of the women was insecure and self-condemning. The opportunity came to speak to her privately and I asked her about it. I said, "Beth (not her real name), I have noticed that you put yourself down a lot and appear to have a feeling of low self-worth." She bowed her head and recounted her strained relationship with her mother. Her mom would say things like, "You will never amount to anything!" or "You will never be good at that." Beth had somehow believed these words and disqualified herself from all that God has declared about who she is in Christ.

I had her read the following material every day for a couple of weeks because it speaks about the way God actually feels about us, according to the Bible. This teaching was a wonderful revelation to her. Many men and women have been strengthened with these truths as they learn their identity in Christ.

This list makes a great guide to pray through personally or corporately!

Who I am in Christ

Biblical Truths to "Practice" Believing

I AM GOD'S . . .

- possession
- child
- workmanship
- friend
- temple
- vessel
- co-laborer
- witness
- soldier
- ambassador
- building
- instrument
- chosen
- beloved
- precious jewel
- candle in a dark place
- city set on a hill
- salt of the earth

I HAVE BEEN . . .

- redeemed by the blood of Jesus
- set free from sin and condemnation
- set free from Satan's control
- set free from Satan's kingdom
- chosen before the foundation of the world
- predestined to be like Jesus
- forgiven of all my trespasses
- cleansed by the blood of the lamb
- given a sound mind
- given the Holy Spirit
- adopted into God's family
- justified freely by His grace
- given all things pertaining to life and godliness
- given great and precious promises
- given authority over all the power of the enemy
- given wisdom

I HAVE . . .

- access to the Father
- a home in heaven waiting for me
- all things in Christ
- a living hope
- an anchor to my soul
- a hope that is steadfast and unmovable
- authority to tread on serpents
- power to witness
- the tongue of the learned
- the mind of Christ
- boldness and access
- peace with God
- faith like a grain of mustard seed

I AM . . .

- complete in Him
- free forever from sin's power
- sanctified and freed for the Master's use
- loved eternally
- eternally kept in the palm of His hand
- kept by the power of God
- not condemned
- one with the Lord
- on my way to heaven
- alive, quickened by His mighty power
- seated with Christ in heavenly places
- the head and not the tail
- light in the darkness
- one of His sheep
- a citizen of heaven
- hidden with Christ in God
- protected from the evil one
- kept by the power of God
- secure in Christ

- set on a Rock
- more than a conqueror
- born again
- a victor
- healed by His stripes
- covered by the blood of Jesus
- sheltered under His wings
- hidden in the secret place of the Almighty

I CAN . . .
- do all things through Christ who strengthens me
- find mercy and grace to help in need
- come boldly to the throne of grace
- quench all the fiery darts of the wicked one
- tread on the serpent
- defeat the enemy
- declare God's truth
- pray always and everywhere
- chase a thousand

I CANNOT . . .
- be separated from God's love
- be lost
- be removed from His grasp
- taken out of the Father's hand

Practice

I often read through this list and thank God for each of the statements He makes about us. I highly recommend that you do the same. If you are short on time, do half the list on one day and the other half on the next. Get His thoughts in your mind. The goal is to think about yourself the way He thinks of you, not the way Satan has been trying to pervert the truth about you.

This list can be used for prayer times in small groups and larger prayer gatherings as well.

Use it regularly and you will begin to see yourself the way God sees you, and you will put away the lies that have followed you for years. Transformation takes place when you replace the lies of the evil one with God's Word. "Therefore, if anyone is in Christ, the new creation has come: The old has gone, the new is here!" (2 Corinthians 5:17)

You know you have it when . . .

You begin to see yourself as God sees you and you can denounce and discard the lies of the enemy that have influenced you.

NOTES

_____

_____

_____

_____

_____

_____

_____

The "Who I AM in Christ" list is developed by Richard LaFountain. It appears with other excellent prayer resources on the website, prayertoday.org, and is used with permission.

CREATIVE WAY

16

Praise

I had an unusual experience one Easter. Each year, at the churches I have served, we invite the members to join us in praying for those who attend our Easter services.

At my last church, we would have as many as 20 services on our five campuses. There was a team of intercessors praying for those attending each service. It is a powerful thing for churches to pray for guests to be drawn to the Father while they are attending a service. Many of our new recruits for intercession have come out of this call to pray for our Easter guests.

At the 4 p.m. service one Easter, we had only people who were brand new to service intercession, show up to pray. This is very rare. We usually have a few experienced intercessors at each service.

I began the prayer time thinking there were some experienced intercessors present. We started our time of prayer with praise. They did their best to praise God but after a couple of minutes they had used every exaltation they could think of.

It became so apparent to me that the church in America is not teaching her people to praise God. I dream of the day when I am in a prayer meeting and the praise time gets so carried away that we don't get to some of the other things we planned on praying about that night.

This week, spend time praising God for everything you can think of. This can be done in your personal prayer times, in a small group, or larger prayer gathering. It might be helpful to make a list of all the qualities of God that you want to lift up before you begin your prayer time.

Here are a few to get you started.

- I praise God that He is able!
- I praise God that He is wise!
- I praise God that He is gentle!
- I praise God for His Church and that the Bible says that, "the gates of hell will not prevail against it."
- I praise God for His Word that cleanses my heart.
- I praise God for His promises.

You know you have it when …

Your praise time lasts longer than a couple of minutes or your corporate praise times are filled with joy and not a season of quietness.

NOTES

Jot down below the praises you enjoyed praying.

_____

_____

_____

_____

_____

_____

_____

_____

CREATIVE WAY

G.E.H.A.R.P

One of the things we help our people learn to do is prayerwalk. This is simply praying while you walk around a neighborhood, community or building. As you walk, what you see can stimulate what you pray.

I picked up an outstanding pattern for prayerwalking from a friend who is working undercover in the Middle East. He calls it G.E.H.A.R.P., which stands for:

G — Glory
E — Expansion
H — Hearts and Minds
A — Authority
R — Revival
P — Prosperity

G: Glory of God

That God would be glorified and exalted and worshiped in this community (Hab. 2:14, Rom. 15:9).

E: Expansion of the Kingdom

That many people in this community will come to salvation, communities of believers be planted, hearts ignited for Christ (Is. 9:7, 2 Cor. 10:15-16).

H: Hearts and Minds

That strongholds and bondages will be lifted from the minds of the people in this place, and that hearts will be stirred with hunger for Jesus and truth (2 Cor. 4:4, Acts 17:11).

A: Authority

Taking authority over strongholds of darkness in that place, speaking prophetic words over the place, releasing visions, dreams, signs and wonders in Jesus' name (Matt. 18:18, James 4:7, 2 Cor. 10:3-5).

R: Revival

That believers living in this area would be awakened by the Holy Spirit, have love and passion stirred in them for the lost, and rise to meet the need in their neighborhoods (Luke 10:2, Ez. 37:10).

P: Prosperity

That God would bring blessing and prosperity to this street/area/region that would show His eternal kindness, demonstrate the blessing of His Kingdom, and cause His people to prosper (Jer. 29:7, Ps. 84:5).

We typically make little flash cards for people to take with them as they are walking. See below for the layout of the cards. Then all they need to do is pray the cards as they walk along.

PRAYER CARDS

G: Glory
Hab. 2:14— For the earth will be filled with the knowledge of the glory of the LORD, as the waters cover the sea.

E: Expansion
2 Cor. 10:15-16— Our area of activity among you will greatly expand, so that we can preach the gospel in the regions beyond you.

H: Hearts and Minds
2 Cor. 4:4— The god of this age has blinded the minds of unbelievers, so that they cannot see the light of the gospel of the glory of Christ.

A: Authority
James 4:7— Submit yourselves, then, to God. Resist the devil, and he will flee from you.

R: Revival
Eph. 1:17— That the glorious Father, may give you the Spirit of wisdom and revelation, so that you may know him better.

P: Prosperity
Jer. 29:7— Seek the peace and prosperity of the city . . . Pray to the LORD for it, because if it prospers, you too will prosper.

Prayerwalking using G.E.H.A.R.P. can also work well in groups, depending on what you are walking around or through.

In many situations—such as a neighborhood or around a school—you will not want to have more than two or three people walking and praying together. The idea is not to draw attention to what you are doing, which could bring nervousness to the inhabitants.

But there are some settings where you might pray together in a larger group—such as praying through a church building or a government property on the National Day of Prayer, etc. In such a group setting, give each person a letter and when the group moves from area to area, the same person prays for God's glory to be exposed. The next person prays over the expansion of His Kingdom etc. We have had wonderful results using this method for prayerwalking.

Practice

This week, try to get out on a prayerwalk three or four times. Use the G.E.H.A.R.P. cards to stimulate your praying. Also, be looking at the neighborhood for things you can pray over. There may be clues of prayer needs in what you see. If you see tricycles and toys in the yard, they have children, so you can pray for the welfare of those young ones. If you see abandoned cars or other broken down items, you may be looking at a family who is facing financial trouble or discouragement. Clues like this will help you pray on the walk, as well as using the G.E.H.A.R.P. cards.

If you or your group really gets into prayerwalking, you can check out the resources at waymakers.org. Waymakers has a "What Would Jesus Pray?" series of booklets designed for prayerwalking. The booklets are loaded with Scripture-based prayers to pray over neighborhoods and cities.

You know you have it when ...

The goal of G.E.H.A.R.P. is to get you started in prayerwalking. You know you have it when you don't need cards anymore; you just listen to the Spirit and pray as you are led.

NOTES

_____

_____

_____

_____

_____

_____

_____

_____

CREATIVE WAY

Confession

One of the types of prayer that has all but been abandoned by the modern Church, is prayers of confession. Yet being in a right standing with God is so crucial for power in prayer! We need to regularly deal with the sin in our life if we want to be effective in intercession.

We practice prayers of confession in our service intercession times each week. (We do it out loud.) At first, this may seem weird but if it is set up right, it is a beautiful part of any prayer time.

I begin by saying, "In the church, we all like to attend cleaned up and looking put together. But the truth is, we are all sinners. So to be authentic, it is healthy to admit our sins and confess them. We are looking for the things that need to be dealt with so that nothing hinders our prayers." You can then have a quiet time of silent prayer while people deal with things before the Lord. There may be times where public confession needs to play a role. James 5 tells us to confess your sins to each other so that healing can come.

Confession is a part of the DNA of the prayer gatherings at my church. I think you will find confession to be helpful in your personal prayer life and at your prayer gatherings as well.

I recommend corporate confession as mentioned above but also private confession. For me, this usually happens at night before I go to sleep. I think through the day and ask the Holy Spirit to remind me of the things I have done wrong so that I can confess them and repent. He is very faithful with His job and some days I have plenty to pray over.

Practice

This week, try personal confession.

Take notes below on what you are learning or insights you gain for these times of confession.

The next time you lead a small group or prayer gathering, I recommend having a time at the beginning for confession. It will change the dynamic of your prayer time.

You know you have it when . . .

Confession is not scary or intimidating but natural and helpful. This takes time but is very attainable.

NOTES

_____

_____

_____

_____

_____

_____

_____

_____

CREATIVE WAY

Listening

Prayer

One of the types of prayer that I am growing in right now is listening prayer. My wife and I have used listening prayer to gain insight on thorny issues like raising our three boys, setting boundaries with friends and loved ones, and seeking direction for the future.

Listening prayer is easy to do. We simply pose a question and ask the Lord to clarify the answer.

Recently, we had a hard season when lots of things broke, and circumstances seemed more difficult than they should have been. We started to wonder why. So we posed a question to the Lord, "Why are all these difficult things happening? Are we in sin or is there something we are missing?" Then we waited and listened for anything that might give us a clue. We listened in our Bible studies, we listened in sermons/teaching we heard, we listened throughout the day, and in our prayer times.

As we listened, some thoughts bubbled to the surface.

1. Following Jesus will cost you something.
2. Many people experience far more trying difficulties than we do, so keep that in mind as you journey through life. Paraphrase: "put on your big boy pants."

3. Greater levels of surrender (we had just taken a significant new step in surrender) will not be ignored by the evil one. He will try his best to discourage us and cause us to give in and retreat. Stand firm!

Listening prayer really helped us clear out the noise in our heads and lock in on the Lord during this season. Remember, the Scripture says, "If any of you lacks wisdom, you should ask God, who gives generously to all without finding fault, and it will be given to you" (James 1:5).

It is very hard to hear the Lord's wisdom unless we make a concerted effort to listen. This requires turning the TV and radio off, putting down the tablet and smart phone, and being still and silent. It also can't be done in minute sound bites. It sometimes requires hour-long chunks of time and multiple occasions.

Practice

Think of two or three things you want to hear from the Lord about. Write them down. Then ask God questions about them. Try listening to the Lord on each one. You can do this alone or with someone you trust.

You know you have it when . . .

Listening prayer is a part of what you do in your prayer times, occasionally. We use it for work settings, gaining insight for the future, relationship issues and in many other areas.

NOTES

_____

_____

_____

_____

_____

_____

CREATIVE WAY

Kingdom

Praying

We all pray many kinds of prayers, including casual prayers like, "God, I am late for the doctor's appointment. Please turn all the lights between here and there green." Or sometimes we pray crisis prayers that have a different kind of urgency: "Oh, no, I have cancer. Please heal me, Lord!"

There is nothing wrong with either kind of prayer, but don't forget to add Kingdom prayers to this mix. Kingdom prayers are prayers that *extend* the Kingdom of God. For example, "God please stop the killing of innocent babies by abortion."

Kingdom prayers take an aspect that is right in the Kingdom of God— and then ask God to make it right here on earth.

Practice

Following are a few Kingdom-prayer starters to try this week. Pray one each day, adding your personal thoughts to the starter. Create Kingdom prayers of your own for the following:

- "God, please stop the terrible practice of sex trafficking in our country and our world."

- "Father, please stop the human injustices carried out by North Korea."
- "God, please help the American Church regain more passion for prayer."
- "Lord, please raise up strong Christian leaders from among our young people to take the Church into the next generation."

You'll know you have it when . . .

Kingdom praying is part of your regular prayer times.

NOTES

_____

_____

_____

_____

_____

_____

_____

_____

CREATIVE WAY

Prayers of Surrender

Recently, I went through a season that was very painful. I manage a property for someone I know. I rented the property to some friends who did not have much money, so I let them in with a very small deposit. Along the way, I made sure that the rent stayed as low as possible. From time to time, I even did some things that, by lease, were to be the tenant's expense, and I did other gestures of kindness to save them time and money.

When they moved out, I discovered that they had not taken care of the place. They had not watered, so the grass was all but dead. There were holes in the walls in the garage. The kitchen counter had a burn mark on it from someone placing a hot pan on the counter. All but two or three light bulbs in the place were burned out, and for some reason they had destroyed nine of the window screens on the house.

All of this was bad, but when I went to settle up with them for the damages, they would not even talk to me. It was obvious that what I thought was friendship was not. I felt hurt and even betrayed.

During the same period, I lost the engine in my truck at 85,000 miles and then four weeks later, the transmission went out.

I was also experiencing some health issues: cancer, atrial fibulation and an auto-immune disorder that was attacking my eyes. The disorder affected my sight and forced me to take chemo drugs to lower the auto-immune reactions indefinitely.

As you can imagine, my load, like yours, gets hard to carry. But I have found a way to help with the emotion pain. I call it "Prayers of Surrender."

What you do is surrender each of the issues you are battling to the Lord one by one. This may be hard at first but it brings great healing. It also may take some time to deal with all of them.

Pray a simple prayer over each circumstance: "Lord, I surrender this situation to You. You are in control. I choose to not worry about it anymore, because I know it is in Your hands."

Our only goal in life is to bring glory to God (1 Cor. 5:8). I forget the goal from time to time, and prayers of surrender help me get back on track.

Practice

Make a list of the things you are struggling with. Then, one by one, surrender them to the Lord and bring them under His Lordship. An extra step you can take is to thank Him for the struggle and place your faith in Him completely to carry you through. Although this is challenging, it is so liberating.

You know you have it when . . .

You feel the freedom that comes from allowing Him to carry your burdens instead of you.

NOTES

_____

_____

_____

_____

_____

_____

CREATIVE WAY

Praying the

Lord's Prayer

Although the Lord's Prayer has been around for a long time, many Christians have not prayed except to pray it in unison in church. I have found joy in breaking it apart and praying the different elements of the Lord's Prayer.

"Our Father" is recognition of our relationship with God. He is our Father. When we had our grandchildren over for a couple of days, I noticed that they did not have a care in the world. They knew Mimi and Popeye would take care of them. There was a special bond and joy in that relationship. This is how it should be with our heavenly Father.

"Who art in Heaven; Hallowed be Thy Name" is worship. Spend some time worshiping and praising God for who He is. I love to praise God. See how long you can come up with qualities that are worthy of praise, and praise Him.

"Your Kingdom come, Your will be done on earth as it is in Heaven" is a call for God's Kingdom to come and manifest itself on earth, just like it is in Heaven. We want to see His reign and rule extended on earth just like it is in heaven because we know the blessing that would bring. Spend some time praying for the fullness of God's Kingdom over your neighborhood, your children's school, your church, your family. The list is unending.

"Give us this day our daily bread" is a call for daily provisions. This is where you ask God to provide for the extra bill that came in unexpectedly, or the cost related to the news that your daughter will be needing braces. Your heavenly Dad loves to know your concerns and He moves when we pray.

"Forgive us our trespasses as we forgive others who trespass against us." Here is the place to ask for forgiveness for the things you have done wrong. List your sins, one at a time, and ask for forgiveness. Then spend some time forgiving those who have wronged you. This is harder, but ensures your forgiveness from God (Matt. 6:12-15, 18:32-35).

"Lead us not into temptation" is a plea for God to prevent temptations from coming our way. Most of our prayers miss this important focus. Ask the Lord to help you with the challenges and wars you will face today and give you victory.

"For yours is the kingdom, the power, and the glory forever and ever." This appeal reminds us of the One we just prayed to and recalibrates our vision. We are praying to the King of Kings and the Creator of all. He does have the power to meet us in our journeys and give us success.

Practice

If you have time, pray each section of the Lord's Prayer daily. I know several national prayer leaders who pray the Lord's Prayer each day. Give it a try.

If you are pressed for time, pray a couple of sections each day. Take notes below on how you did and breakthroughs you experienced.

This can also be used as a prayer time in a small group or larger prayer gathering. Simply guide your people through each phrase, having them pray what is on their heart related to each section.

You know you have it when . . .

The Lord's Prayer is not just a nice prayer to hang on the wall, but a powerful plea before our Father.

NOTES

_____

_____

_____

_____

_____

_____

_____

_____

CREATIVE WAY

Praying the

Names of God

Have you ever prayed the names of God? There are lots of them and each one helps us to fully appreciate who God is.

In your personal prayer life, one of the best ways to start is to think of a specific situation in which you need God's help. What characteristics do you need that are implied in a specific name (healing, comfort, etc.)? Start praying that name over your situation.

Here are a few to get you started:

Bread of Life	King of Kings	Rock
Wonderful Counselor	Mighty Warrior	Redeemer
Healer	Provider	Light
Comforter	Friend	Brother
Protector	The Way, the Truth, and the Life	Judge
Head of the Church	Prince of Peace	Able

Practice

Pick out a couple of these for each day and pray them. Thank God for who He is and what He does for us.

In a small group or prayer gathering, you can easily adapt this for use. Provide a handout of names or put them on a screen and have people pray prayers either of praise, declaring that name, or prayers that call on the power of that name in a given situation.

You know you have it when . . .

You find names of God in your Bible and you begin to incorporate them into your prayer times. As you read your Bible, look for other names for God that you can pray. Your list should get very long and helpful.

NOTES

_____

_____

_____

_____

_____

_____

_____

_____

CREATIVE WAY

Writing Out

Your Prayers

While in Bible college, one of the professors I respected most always encouraged us to write out, in longhand, our prayers to God. I remember seeing a10-inch stack of paper in his office, which were his written prayers.

There are many advantages in writing out your prayers:

- It is harder for your mind to wander when you write out your prayers.
- You remember what you asked God for more clearly if you exert the effort to write out your prayers.
- You have a record of what you prayed and when you prayed it to review.

One of the joys of my life is when I take a day occasionally to revisit my Bible studies and past written prayers. I am astounded at the ways God prepared me for what I couldn't see yet.

You will notice His loving hand orchestrating your life and meeting you personally if you have a record like this. You will see prayers that were answered in ways you never dreamed.

Practice

During this next week, take the time to write out your prayers each day. If typing is easier, use your computer but write them out in full. Then at the end of the week, look back over what you prayed and look for places where God met you in those prayers. Jot down what you learn in the note section that follows.

You will know you have it when . . .

You have a record of what you have prayed and can see the hand of God moving in your prayer.

We record things that are important to us. We record birthdays, social security numbers, wedding anniversaries, and bank account numbers. But for most of us, there is no record of the prayers we have prayed or what we have asked God for. Having that kind of record could prove revolutionary in your life.

NOTES

_____

_____

_____

_____

_____

_____

_____

_____

CREATIVE WAY

Declarative

Prayers

Declarative prayers are declarations of God's truth. Each time a prayer is prayed, we use the phrase, "I declare that God is _____."

Here are a few examples:
- God, I declare that You are able!
- God, I declare that Your wisdom is unsearchable!
- God, I declare that You are the King of Kings and Lord of Lords!
- God, I declare that the gates of hell will not prevail against Your Church!
- God, I declare that You are a victorious God!

This can be done personally or in a small group. Either way, the outcome is the same. One declaration builds on the next and before long you can visibly see people sitting up taller and walking in the truths they are declaring.

Practice
I recommend you practice declarative prayer in a personal setting and if

possible in a small group setting. It is extremely powerful and empowering.

You know you have it when . . .

You find yourself praying declaratory prayers frequently and teaching others to do so also.

NOTES

Jot down some of your favorite declarations here.

CREATIVE WAY

Praying

Jesus

Have you ever thought about using the body of Jesus as prayer prompts—His eyes, ears, hands, arms, or feet? I have found great comfort in doing this as I pray over myself or others.

If you are in a situation where you don't know what to do, for instance, pray like this, "Jesus, I know You can see things I will never see. So I am asking You to give me Your eyes in this situation so I will know what You want me do—and do it with confidence." Identify with Jesus in a personal way that prompts you to pray creatively.

Practice

Pray for:
- His ears to hear what only He can hear.
- His hands to help another.
- His feet to flee from temptation.
- His eyes to see the way He sees.
- His mind to give you the wisdom you need.
- His mind/thoughts to speak the right words.

- His smile to comfort another.
- His attitude in the midst of suffering.

You'll know you have it when . . .

You find comfort in the presence of Jesus and all His abilities and personal characteristics.

NOTES

_____

_____

_____

_____

_____

_____

_____

_____

CREATIVE WAY

3 X 5 Cards

One of the hardest parts of prayer is thinking through precisely what you want to pray about for each person on your list.

My wife and I have found a method of prayer that works really well for us. We use 3 x 5 cards. We have a card for each other, our children, parents, and grandkids. Each card has detailed and specific prayer requests for that person.

We can use these cards when we pray alone or together. When together, we each select two or three cards from the ones we have already prepared and we pray those cards. Next time we choose two or three different cards. Using this method makes sure we are praying with forethought and that each loved one gets careful prayer.

Practice

Buy a package of 3 x 5 cards and make a list of friends and family you want to pray for. Then use the cards to write out the specific requests you want to pray for each person. In time you will find the need to add requests for some of your people and delete some requests that have been answered. Make a set of 3 x 5 cards for your loved ones and give this method of prayer a try this week.

Small Group Use

A variation of this can be used in a small group. Bring a pack of cards and have each member of the group write down their name on a card and a Scripture verse they would like to have prayed for them. Shuffle the cards and give one to each. Then pray. Or give out with the idea that this week each person prays for the person whose card they received.

You know you have it when . . .

The people you care about are being prayed for specifically and consistently in a fashion that is manageable.

NOTES

_____

_____

_____

_____

_____

_____

_____

_____

CREATIVE WAY

Prayers of

Perseverance

I was teaching a life group recently on perseverance in prayer. I shared Luke 7:37-38: "A woman in that town who lived a sinful life learned that Jesus was eating at the Pharisee's house, so she came there with an alabaster jar of perfume. As she stood behind him at his feet weeping, she began to wet his feet with her tears. Then she wiped them with her hair, kissed them and poured perfume on them."

We discussed her stunning adoration of Jesus.

I believe that some of the greatest worship we do (like this sinful woman) is continuing to pray for something even when we can't see any movement. As we keep trusting and praying, we are anointing Jesus afresh with the costly perfume of worship.

As I was talking, one of the couples was visibly shaken by my words and the woman began to cry. I noted that I must have touched a nerve and asked why the strong response. The couple told me they have a son who has had heart trouble since birth. He has had surgery after surgery and it has been a rough road. As I was speaking, they began to see their yet unanswered prayers for their son in the way I was presenting them. They for the first time saw their prayers for their son as an exquisite offering of love to the Savior.

I challenge you to continue praying some of those prayers you have been praying for a long time. Pray them not as drudgery, but as offerings of worship and unconditional love.

Practice

Make a list below of the prayers that you need to keep on praying even though you have seen no movement. Commit to continuing to pray those prayers daily this week and to view them as some of your best worship to the Father.

You know you have it when . . .

You find the prayers that need continual praying are stepping stones to great worship.

NOTES

_____

_____

_____

_____

_____

_____

_____

_____

CREATIVE WAY

Reading Your

Prayers

A popular phrase when it comes to learning to pray is "Prayer is caught, not taught." That means sometimes we learn a lot from hearing others pray. Praying the prayers of Scripture, or using a prayer guide that has Scripture-based prayer written out already, can make us more effective intercessors.

This week I have selected seven great prayers or Scriptures to pray. Read, pray and ponder one each day.

The Lord's Prayer

"Our Father in heaven, hallowed be your name, your kingdom come, your will be done, on earth as it is in heaven. Give us today our daily bread. And forgive us our debts, as we also have forgiven our debtors. And lead us not into temptation, but deliver us from the evil one." (Matthew 6:9-13)

Twenty-Third Psalm

"The LORD is my shepherd, I lack nothing. He makes me lie down in green pastures, he leads me beside quiet waters, he refreshes my soul. He guides me along the right paths for his name's sake. Even though I walk through the darkest valley, I will fear no evil, for you are with me; your rod and your staff, they comfort me. You prepare a table before me in the presence of my enemies. You anoint my head with oil; my cup overflows. Surely your goodness and love will follow me all the days of my life, and I will dwell in the house of the LORD forever." (Psalms 23:1-6)

Make Me an Instrument of Your Peace

Lord, make me an instrument of your peace.
Where there is hatred, let me sow love,
Where there is injury, pardon,
Where there is doubt, faith,
Where there is despair, hope,
Where there is darkness, light,
Where there is sadness, joy.
O Divine Master, grant that I may not so much
seek to be consoled as to console,
not so much to be understood as to understand,
not so much to be loved, as to love;
for it is in giving that we receive,
it is in pardoning that we are pardoned,
it is in dying that we awake to eternal life.

—St. Francis of Assisi

David's Prayer of Repentance, Psalm 51

"Have mercy on me, O God, according to your unfailing love; according to your great compassion blot out my transgressions. Wash away all my iniquity and cleanse me from my sin."

"For I know my transgressions, and my sin is always before me. Against you, you only, have I sinned and done what is evil in your sight; so you are right in your verdict and justified when you judge. Surely I was sinful at birth, sinful from the time my mother conceived me. Yet you desired faithfulness even in the womb; you taught me wisdom in that secret place. Cleanse me with hyssop, and I will be clean; wash me, and I will be whiter than snow. Let me hear joy and gladness; let the bones you have crushed rejoice. Hide your face from my sins and blot out all my iniquity. Create in me a pure heart, O God, and renew a steadfast spirit within me. Do not cast me from your presence or take your Holy Spirit from me. Restore to me the joy of your salvation and grant me a willing spirit, to sustain me. Then I will teach transgressors your ways, so that sinners will turn back to you. Deliver me from the guilt of bloodshed, O God, you who are God my Savior, and my tongue will sing of your righteousness. Open my lips, Lord, and my mouth will declare your praise. You do not delight in sacrifice, or I would bring it; you do not take pleasure in burnt offerings. My sacrifice, O God, is a broken spirit; a broken and contrite heart you, God, will not despise." (Psalms 51:1-17)

Daniel's Prayer of Repentance, Daniel 9
I prayed to the LORD my God and confessed: "LORD, the great and awesome God, who keeps his covenant of love with those who love him and keep his commandments, we have sinned and done wrong. We have been wicked and have rebelled; we have turned away from your commands and laws. We have not listened to your servants the prophets, who spoke in your name to our kings, our princes and our ancestors, and to all the people of the land.

"Lord, you are righteous, but this day we are covered with shame—the people of Judah and the inhabitants of Jerusalem and all Israel, both near and far, in all the countries where you have scattered us because of our unfaithfulness to you. We and our kings, our princes and our ancestors are covered with shame, LORD, because we have sinned against you. The Lord our God is merciful and forgiving, even though we have rebelled against him; we have not obeyed the LORD our God or kept the laws he gave us through his servants the prophets. All Israel has transgressed your law and turned away, refusing to obey you.

"Therefore the curses and sworn judgments written in the Law of Moses, the servant of God, have been poured out on us, because we have sinned against you. You have fulfilled the words spoken against us and against our rulers by bringing on us great disaster. Under the whole heaven nothing has ever been done like what has been done to Jerusalem. Just as it is written in the Law of Moses, all this disaster has come on us, yet we have not sought the favor of the LORD our God by turning from our sins and giving attention to your truth. The LORD did not hesitate to bring the disaster on us, for the LORD our God is righteous in everything he does; yet we have not obeyed him.

"Now, LORD our God, who brought your people out of Egypt with a mighty hand and who made for yourself a name that endures to this day, we have sinned, we have done wrong. Lord, in keeping with all your righteous acts, turn away your anger and your wrath from Jerusalem, your city, your holy hill. Our sins and the iniquities of our ancestors have made Jerusalem and your people an object of scorn to all those around us.

"Now, our God, hear the prayers and petitions of your servant. For your sake, Lord, look with favor on your desolate sanctuary. Give ear, our God, and hear; open your eyes and see the desolation of the city that bears your Name. We do not make requests of you because we are righteous, but because of your great mercy. Lord, listen! Lord, forgive! Lord, hear and act! For your sake, my God, do not delay, because your city and your people bear your Name." (Daniel 9:4-19)

Paul's Prayer for the Ephesian Church
"For this reason I kneel before the Father, from whom every family in heaven and on earth derives its name. I pray that out of his glorious riches he may strengthen you with power through his Spirit in your inner being, so that Christ may dwell in your hearts through faith. And I pray that you, being rooted and established in love, may have power, together with all the Lord's holy people, to grasp how wide and long and high and deep is the love of Christ, and to know this love that surpasses knowledge—that you may be filled to the measure of all the fullness of God.

"Now to him who is able to do immeasurably more than all we ask or imagine, according to his power that is at work within us, to him be glory in the church and in Christ Jesus throughout all generations, for ever and ever! Amen." (Ephesians 3:16-21)

Jesus' Prayer of Submission
"He withdrew about a stone's throw beyond them, knelt down and prayed,

'Father, if you are willing, take this cup from me; yet not my will, but yours be done.'" (Luke 22:41-42)

You know you have it when . . .

Praying the prayers of others can be part of the way you pray from time to time.

NOTES

_____

_____

_____

_____

_____

_____

_____

_____

CREATIVE WAY

Jericho

March

There is a kind of prayer that I am late in learning. It is called prophetic prayer.

I first experienced this brand of praying at a prayer conference for the nations. The prayer leader had all the men circle the auditorium and pretend they had nets in their hands. They were to throw the nets in the imaginary water and pull in the catch of fish. The fish represented the lost in the world; we were particularly focused on the lost in the Middle East.

The women stood in the center of the circle and were to walk toward the men symbolically driving the fish toward the nets. Then sincere prayer was offered for the world's unreached peoples.

You remember Joshua's siege of Jericho in Joshua 6. He had the people march around the city once each day. They were led by the Ark of the Covenant and seven priests blowing trumpets. On the seventh day, they trudged around the city seven times. Then at the signal, they shouted loudly and blew their trumpets. As a result, the walls of the city collapsed.

Jericho was a city that needed to be captured but it was well reinforced and seemed impregnable. God used this unconventional means of battle to ensure that everyone knew He was the conqueror.

Similarly, sometimes the battles we face in life are large and looming. Prophetic prayer takes a biblical story or scene and calls people to stand on the faith seen in the story for their situation.

Try walking around a job location each day and asking God to give you your dream job in that location. How about striding around a business that has wronged you and requesting that God hear your cry for justice? Do you have a friend who is involved in court proceedings? Consider a "Jericho March" around the courthouse asking God for impartiality and truth to be known in your friend's case.

The list of these is endless so have fun and be creative.

This method of prayer can be used in groups also.

At one of the churches I worked we surrounded and walked the property with church members and prayed for what God was going to do on the land we were preparing to build on. It was powerful.

One of the churches where I work does the Jericho March once a month over the prayer requests they receive. They place all the prayer cards on the table and then each member prays over a card as they walk around the table. When they have finished that card, they pick up another and pray over it until they have prayed over all cards. They pray out loud all at the same time. It is a wonderful way to add variety to the prayer room.

Practice

There seems to be something faith building about taking a biblical story and standing on that miracle as we pray for our present needs. Jericho Marches can be very encouraging. Look for a situation in which you can experiment with prophetic prayer and a Jericho March.

You know you have it when . . .

You have developed an ability to pray prophetic prayers, based on Scripture, and they increase your faith and the faith of others.

NOTES

CREATIVE WAY

31

Praying for

Government Leaders

O fficials in all levels of government have huge roles to play and require great wisdom. One of the best things we can do is to pray for them. Most of us do that from time to time if we remember, or if we become aware of an important issue that is up for a vote, but what would happen if we all made praying for government officials a semi-regular part of our prayer life?

I encourage you to make a list of things you can pray for . . .
- Local officials such as mayor, city council, police chief, etc.
- State officials such as senators, congressmen or women, governor, etc.
- National leaders

What could you pray?
- Look for issues they are being called to weigh in on and pray over those issues.
- Ask God to make them men and women of integrity.
- Pray for their protection.

- Pray for a desire to work with other political leaders to get the job done instead of partisan politics.
- Pray for their spiritual walks. Ask God to bring them to Christ if they do not yet know Him, and for those who are believers, pray that they would walk in a manner worthy of their calling in Christ.

Practice

Consider expanding your list to include judges, city councils, major spiritual leaders in your city and other key leaders.

You know you have it when . . .

You are praying for Kingdom issues in your city, state, nation and these kinds of prayers are part of your consistent prayers.

NOTES

CREATIVE WAY

Praying for a

Loved One

When I speak, I find that it is pretty easy to convince people of the power of prayer. But although they are convinced, they often don't know where or how to start. So I created this diagram to meet that need.

Begin by listening to God about those for whom you want to pray. God knows what your loved one needs better than you do. So take a few minutes to ask Him what to pray, then listen for His response. After you have heard from God, move to praying for your loved ones' spiritual health, then their physical needs. Next, for their relationships.

The next three are a little deeper. Pray for your loved ones' purposes in life, the strongholds they battle with, and finally pray in detail for them. Do they need a job? Are they unwilling to forgive right now? Do they need to come to faith? All of these go under the heading of specific targets for your loved one.

Practice

Use this diagram all week to pray for one or more loved ones.

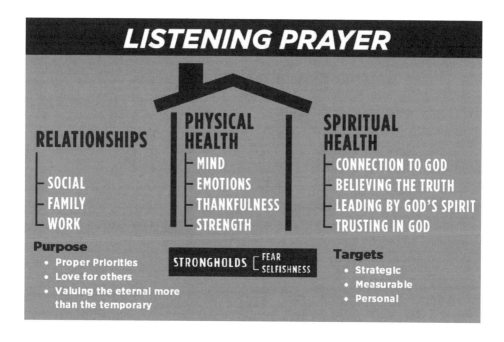

LISTENING PRAYER

RELATIONSHIPS
- SOCIAL
- FAMILY
- WORK

PHYSICAL HEALTH
- MIND
- EMOTIONS
- THANKFULNESS
- STRENGTH

SPIRITUAL HEALTH
- CONNECTION TO GOD
- BELIEVING THE TRUTH
- LEADING BY GOD'S SPIRIT
- TRUSTING IN GOD

Purpose
- Proper Priorities
- Love for others
- Valuing the eternal more than the temporary

STRONGHOLDS
- FEAR
- SELFISHNESS

Targets
- Strategic
- Measurable
- Personal

You Know you have it when . . .

You are praying strategically for your loved ones.

NOTES

_____

_____

_____

_____

_____

_____

_____

_____

CREATIVE WAY

Praying

the News

This week, the assignment is to pray about the things that are going on in the world around you. To do this you will need to watch, read, or listen to the news. Select the way that is most convenient for you to gather what is happening in the world: online, TV, or from the newspaper.

Make notes of the stories that touch your heart or that concern you. Pray over them this week.

As you ponder what to pray over them, remember these three truths:

- God's ways are higher than our ways.
- God desires all men to come to a knowledge of the truth.
- God desires to bring glory to His Son, Jesus.

So when you pray, rather than just pray the obvious things over a news story, ponder what God might be doing to draw people to Himself and to give glory to His Son. Pray for that to happen!

Practice

Record several issues here that you want to pray and watch for God's movement.

You know you have it when . . .

You spontaneously pray over news items whenever or wherever you hear, see, or read them.

NOTES

Write down any notes or thoughts you have this week as you pray about the news.

_____

_____

_____

_____

_____

_____

_____

_____

CREATIVE WAY
34

Forgiveness Prayers

F orgiveness is spoken of often in the Scriptures—both the gift of the forgiveness of our sins by God, and our need to forgive others who have wronged us.

In the Lord's Prayer, Jesus tied the two together saying that if we did not forgive others their trespasses against us, God would not forgive us (Matt. 6:12-14). But beyond the spiritual ramifications of forgiveness, there is a lot of research that shows a physical result when we do not forgive.

Unforgiveness is classified in medical books as a disease. According to Dr. Steven Standiford, chief of surgery at the Cancer Treatment Centers of America, refusing to forgive makes people sick and keeps them that way. . . .

Of all cancer patients, 61 percent have forgiveness issues, and of those, more than half are severe, according to research by Dr. Michael Barry, a pastor and the author of the book, *The Forgiveness Project*. . . .

Harboring these negative emotions, this anger and hatred, creates a state of chronic anxiety, he said. Chronic anxiety very predictably produces excess adrenaline and cortisol, which deplete the production of natural killer cells, which is your body's foot soldier in the fight against cancer, he explained. . . .

Barry said, "Most people don't realize what a burden anger and hatred were until they let them go." . . .

—Taken from "The Deadly Consequences of Unforgiveness" by Lorie Johnson, Christian Broadcasting Network News. June 22, 2015.

That's why it is extremely important to be regularly dealing with forgiveness in our own lives—so we can be spiritually fit and physically fit.

This week's prayer is a prayer of forgiveness. First, get before the Lord and ask Him directly, "Is there someone who wronged me who I have not forgiven?" Then listen and document the names of people you need to forgive.

Next, forgive them one at a time in prayer. Verbally tell the Lord that you forgive this person and will no longer hold over them what they did. "And when you stand praying, if you hold anything against anyone, forgive them, so that your Father in heaven may forgive you your sins" (Mark 11:25).

With very difficult situations sometimes I have forgiven with a witness who observes my prayer of forgiveness. This has proven helpful with the tough prayers of forgiveness.

Practice

When the Lord reveals someone who you need to forgive, take time to forgive them each day this week, or until you feel release from the situation.

You know you have it when . . .

You don't carry around resentments and bitterness. You have learned in the future to let things go quickly.

NOTES

Record your feeling and the results of your prayers of forgiveness in the space provided below.

_____

_____

_____

_____

CREATIVE WAY

"Open My Eyes"

Prayers

Sometimes our problems in life seem so large we don't know what to do.

That was the case in 2 Kings 6: 15-17. The king of Aram was so frustrated with the Prophet Elisha and his ability to warn Israel of Aramean surprise attacks, that he sent his army by night to surround the city of Dothan, where Elisha lived, intending to capture him. When Elisha's servant saw the vast army, he panicked. The man of God was not fearful at all but prayed that God would, "Open his (servant's) eyes so that he may see." When the Lord opened the servant's eyes, he looked and saw the hills full of horses and chariots of fire all around Elisha. The Lord gave Elisha's servant the ability to perceive the normally unseen world of invisible spirits (angels) that were ready to do His bidding. How opened eyes changes the picture! What a great prayer to pray this week.

Practice

What are the things and situations that are weighing on you this week? Ask the Lord to open your eyes in those areas to see what He is doing. Think of areas like work, school, family, relationships, problems, and even successes.

As He begins to give you a sense of what He is doing, or He gives you a peace that He is in control, begin to praise Him. If He gives you a sense of what He is going to do, thank Him and pray for that to come to pass.

You know you have it when . . .
The "open my eyes" kind of prayer is a standard in your private prayer times.

NOTES

_____

_____

_____

_____

_____

_____

_____

_____

CREATIVE WAY

36

"Even If" Prayers

One of my favorite places in the Old Testament is 2 Kings 7.

The Aramean army laid siege to a city in Samaria. That plus a horrible famine in the land made conditions in the city hopeless from any human perspective. Enter Elisha the prophet of God, who matter-of-factly predicts that tomorrow at this time, food would be in abundance.

As you follow the story, the king's officer hears the prediction and states, "*Even if* the Lord should open the windows of heaven, this prediction could not come to pass." In the meantime four lepers make the decision to go over the Aramean camp. They surmise, that if they stay there, they will die of starvation. But if they go over to the enemy camp, the enemy may have pity on them, spare them and give them something to eat.

When the lepers arrive in the Aramean camp, they learn that God had caused the Arameans to hear the sounds of chariots, horses and a great army. The soldiers had become so afraid that they had dropped everything and fled. The lepers begin to feast on the spoils left behind in the camp.

Finally, they become convicted that the others in the city are still starving and decide to go back and tell them of their good fortune. When the people hear of the food and spoil available in the Aramean camp, they stampede out of the city and the officer of the king who questioned Elisha's prediction is trampled to death!

There are several other "even if" stands in the Scripture:

- Shadrach, Meshach and Abednego, facing the fiery furnace, proclaimed, "But *even if* [God does not save us from the furnace] we want you to know, your Majesty, that we will not serve your gods or worship your image of gold you have set up" (Dan. 3:18).
- Queen Esther made the choice to have faith as her people were about to be destroyed by wicked Haman. She was willing to move forward *even if* it cost her very life (see book of Esther).
- Mary was willing to surrender to God unconditionally when she became aware of His plan to have her bear the Son of God, even though she was unwed and would experience ridicule (see Luke 1:26-38).

Do you have a situation or struggle that seems impossible? Will you step forward in faith and pray the *even if* prayer?

- Lord, *even if* this does not work out the way I want it to, I will not stop trusting You.
- Lord, *even if* this causes me more pain, I will trust You.

Practice

Write down some places in your life you need some "*even if*" faith and prayer below. Then begin to pray prayers of faith over those situations.

You know you have when . . .

There is no prayer that seems impossible to you.

NOTES

Record your thoughts and victories in the space below.

_____

_____

_____

_____

_____

_____

CREATIVE WAY

Prayer for the

Nations

As we mature in prayer, one of the things God will ask us to begin praying for is "the nations." Why? Because of His purposes for the world.

There is a verse in Psalms (2:8) that has challenged me for years. It is "Ask me, and I will make the nations your inheritance, the ends of the earth your possession." It appears to me that God is calling us to pray for the nations of the earth. It also appears in some mysterious way He has limited Himself to act, at least in part, to the prayers of His people. So Psalm 2:8 is a clarion call to pray for the nations.

Practice

This week, pick out either seven countries that you want to pray for, or one country that you would pray for seven times. Ask God to lay a nation or nations on your heart. What nation in the news seems to draw your interest?

Then spend your prayer time praying for things like:

- Governments to open to the gospel.
- The churches in the country to be an outstanding light for the nation.
- Safety for believers in the country.

- Barriers to be removed that prevent the gospel from being shared.
- Ask God for a move of harvest in the countries you selected.
- Christian workers in country to be insightful and diligent in how they do their work.
- Ask God to protect the marriages of the Christian workers in the nations you were drawn to.

Listen to the Lord about any other specific items to be lifted up and include those in your prayers. You can record your insights below.

You know you have it when . . .
You begin to develop a heart for the nations of the world.

NOTES

_____

_____

_____

_____

_____

_____

_____

_____

CREATIVE WAY

38

Praying for Unity

Unity is important to God. Especially unity between brothers and sisters in Christ. Psalm 133:1 says, "How good and pleasant it is when God's people live together in unity!" Jesus prayed for unity in His Last Supper prayer where He prayed for the disciples . . . and us, future disciples.

I pray also for those who will believe in me through their message, that all of them may be one, Father, just as you are in me and I am in you. May they also be in us so that the world may believe that you have sent me. I have given them the glory that you gave me, that they may be one as we are one—I in them and you in me—so that they may be brought to complete unity. Then the world will know that you sent me and have loved them even as you have loved me. (John 17:21-23)

Since unity is so important to Jesus, we should pray for it, too. When was the last time you prayed for unity? The truth is that the body of Christ is fractured over and over again by judgments, hurtful statements, pride, ego and selfishness.

We need an army of people in the Church praying for unity! Pray daily for unity in your church and between the churches in your community.

But we also should be praying for the places where we bring disunity! I was meditating on this recently and a thought came to me, *Oh Lord where am I hurting unity and breaking Your heart?*

This week, pray for unity among others you know in the body of Christ. Look for those you have had a "run in" with and ask God to make those relationships new. Pray for those who have overlooked you and pray that you will not be so petty. Don't stop until you have covered each item the Lord brings to your mind.

Practice

Add a cry for unity for your church to your prayers!

Also, on a personal level, ask the Lord to reveal any situation where you sowed disunity and write it below. Then begin to pray over each one until you have a heart of unity and love. Don't compromise here. Clear up each one.

You know you have it when . . .

There is no one whom you have anything against and no one who has something against you. When your emotional reservoir is clean and pure with no imperfections.

NOTES

_____

_____

_____

_____

_____

_____

_____

_____

CREATIVE WAY

39

Pray at a

Specific Time

Acts 3:1 tells us, "One day Peter and John were going up to the temple at the time of prayer—at three in the afternoon." Evidently, the early church had set a time during their day to pray.

While you may have a regular time that you pray, like when you first wake up, I encourage you from time to time to practice setting your alarm to a specific time each day where you intend to pray for something specific.

Several of my pastor friends have set an alarm for specific times of the day to pray. They actually pick a time based on a specific verse. One friend sets his alarm to 4:31 p.m. This time comes from Acts 4:31: "After they prayed, the place where they were meeting was shaken." He prays for His church to be full of the Holy Spirit.

Another prays for lost friends at 2:41 p.m. "Those who accepted his message were baptized, and about three thousand were added to their number that day" (Acts 2:41).

Pick a time that you want to pray and a specific focus over which you will pray (the time may or may not relate to a verse reference). Then set your phone alarm or another alarm to ring daily. When it rings, take a few minutes and pray. This is a great way to keep you grounded in the middle of a hectic day.

This practice can also be used in a small group if you all decide to pray at a certain time for a specific item. I still encourage you to select a verse to pray in this situation.

Practice

Spend some time to find a verse that is meaningful to you and then set your alarm. Begin praying each day at that time. Obviously, if the reference is not convenient due to work or family responsibilities, you can pick any time.

You know you have it when . . .

Praying at a certain time becomes part of your prayer routine.

NOTES

_____

_____

_____

_____

_____

_____

_____

_____

CREATIVE WAY

A Place to Pray

In Acts 16:16 it appears that Paul and Silas, while in Philippi, selected a specific place of prayer or decided to go to a place that had been designated as a place of prayer. "Once when we were going to the place of prayer, we were met by a female slave who . . . "

I have been to the spot where scholars believe Paul and Silas gathered for prayer in Philippi. It was a beautiful stream surrounded by lush trees.

In my own prayer life, I have found that having a specific place of prayer can be powerful and even critical in connecting with God. If you do not already have one, I recommend considering a specific place you can designate as "my prayer place."

There are several things that are a must in selecting a place of prayer:

- It needs to be a place where you will not be interrupted.
- A spot where you do not have distractions is also helpful. I have tried to pray at my desk in the office. It can be done, but it is difficult. As I am praying, I am reminded of things I need to do at work which derails my prayer time. So a spot away from my work seems to work best for me. Unless you use a Bible app on your phone or tablet, I recommend not having them in your place, or you will get distracted by them.
- It is vital to have a comfortable chair to sit in.

- A view can be very helpful and inspiring if you are lucky enough to have a spot with a vista.
- Music helps some people to focus in their place of prayer with connection to God. I have visited the International House of Prayer in Kansas City. They live stream their prayer room and that helps me to get in the right frame of mind to pray if I am struggling. Watching for 20 minutes helps me immensely. You can find it at ihopkc.org/prayerroom.

Practice

This week, pick a place of prayer and get it set up so you are prepared for earnest prayer. It can be a recliner with a light to read by, or a closet that you have turned into a prayer closet. But whatever you select, get it ready for prayer and to meet God!

You know you have it when . . .
You long to be in that spot to spend time with your Father.

NOTES

_____
_____
_____
_____
_____
_____
_____
_____

CREATIVE WAY

Open Doors

In several places, the New Testament illustrates the concept of opening doors by prayer.

Paul in Colossians 4:3 asked for prayer that doors would be open for the advancement of the gospel, "And pray for us, too, that God may **open a door for our message,** so that we may proclaim the mystery of Christ, for which I am in chains."

Acts chapter 12 records Peter's miraculous escape from prison. You may recall the story. Herod had Peter arrested, bound him with two chains, and Peter was guarded by four squads of soldiers. The church had gathered at Mary's house to pray for him. That night, an angel awakened Peter and his chains fell off. He walked through the prison, past the guards, and the scripture says the **iron gate swung open by itself** to set him free.

In Acts 16:25-27, Paul and Silas were praying and singing in a prison cell in Philippi. "About midnight Paul and Silas were praying and singing hymns to God, and the other prisoners were listening to them. Suddenly there was such a violent earthquake that the foundations of the prison were shaken. **At once all the prison doors flew open, and everyone's chains came loose.** The jailer woke up, and when he saw the prison doors open, he drew his sword and was about to kill himself because he thought the prisoners had escaped."

Praying for doors to open is a biblical practice. What doors do you personally need to see open? How about doors that need to open for your church or friends?

I visited Kosovo years ago. Our workers there are wonderful and faithful, but the work among Muslims was slow at that time. If I remember correctly, the Sunday we were there, 20 believers were in church and that included those on our team and the workers' family. I thought I would be so discouraged if I had put in five years and only had 10 converts. At that time, I began praying regularly with others that the doors would fling open for their ministry . . . and it has through the years.

They are now operating a prestigious Christian School in the region and my friend has been asked by leaders of the nation to help them in a number of areas. His wife runs a medical clinic and it is thriving. Doors have absolutely opened for these faithful servants. Praise God!

Practice

Pray for doors to open in ministries you know about locally, around the world or in your own life. Also pray this prayer for those you love or for yourself, personally.

While we may not have physical chains like Paul and Silas, many of us have spiritual and emotional chains that keep us from moving forward spiritually. Ask God to release you or release those you love from the chains that hold them down.

You know you have it when . . .

You are praying for openings and seeing some of the chains fall off.

NOTES

_____

_____

_____

_____

_____

CREATIVE WAY

"Rapid Fire"

Prayer

I like to invite my church to pray over topics like unity in the Body or national disasters like hurricanes or earthquakes. It is good for the church to pray over these areas.

One of the ways we pray is what I call "Rapid Fire" prayers.

We will set up two microphones, one on either side of the church, and invite people to come to the front and pray over the topic. The idea is for each person to pray 30 seconds and no more. The prayers go "rapid fire" from one side of the church, then the other, and back and forth. Sometimes with newer groups, I will station a prayer leader at each mic so if someone begins to drone over the time limit, they can be gently preempted.

Practice

Try this method with your small group or some friends. Pick a topic and begin to do rapid fire prayer. Prayers will begin to surface that you have never thought of and the topic gets prayed over beautifully.

You know you have it when . . .

Your people are "all in" to the rapid fire kind of prayer and their prayers together make a beautiful expression to God.

NOTES

_____

_____

_____

_____

_____

_____

_____

_____

CREATIVE WAY

B.L.E.S.S.

A friend of mine, Alvin VanderGriend, has come up with a wonderful way to pray for neighbors, friends, or even family. He has devised a prayer pattern using the acronym B.L.E.S.S. What makes his acronym so helpful is we literally are blessing people with prayer. His acronym stimulates prayer over every area of need for another person. I love using this method to pray for others.

I encourage you to pick a few people you can begin to B.L.E.S.S.

PRAY

B - Body: Pray for good health, protection, and strength.

L - Labor: Pray for their work experience and their financial security.

E - Emotional: Pray for emotional health and a good quality of life; for joy, peace, hope.

S - Social: Pray for their relationships with their family and friends.

S - Spiritual: Pray for their salvation, that they will come to faith in Jesus Christ.

—Adopted from "5 Blessings" by Alvin VanderGriend

(Used with Permission)

Practice

Use this prayer model and find someone each day that you can pray for and B.L.E.S.S.

You know you have it when . . .

You can use this model any time or anywhere. Frankly, I use it repeatedly when I am called to pray for others.

NOTES

_____

_____

_____

_____

_____

_____

_____

_____

CREATIVE WAY

Pray for Extended

Family and Friends

Occasionally, I will just use my prayer time to pray for people that I don't pray for on a regular basis. I ask the Lord to bring to mind friends or extended family who need prayer. He is so faithful to do just that. People will begin to pop into my mind that I have not thought about recently. I begin praying and the time flies by.

Paul encouraged us to pray for each other in Ephesians 1:15-16, "For this reason, ever since I heard about your faith in the Lord Jesus and your love for all God's people, I have not stopped giving thanks for you, remembering you in my prayers."

Practice

Quiet your mind and ask the Lord to bring to mind people for whom He wants you to pray. Make a list before you pray or as you are praying so you can recall those for whom you prayed. Continue praying for these friends or family members this week.

You know you have it when . . .

You occasionally make the opportunity to pray for many who are not on your normal prayer list.

NOTES

CREATIVE WAY

Prayer

Texting

A lot of individuals and churches make use of email to send prayer requests or reminders to pray. But by far, the most effective use of technology is to text people. While fewer and fewer people open and read emails quickly or at all (due to the high volume of emails everyone receives), almost 100% of people read their texts.

We have found that texting a prayer can be very effective. People are on their phones all the time and a quick text with a prayer gets their attention almost immediately.

More and more churches are using this form of contact to great success. At Easter time, my church developed "40 Days of Prayer" texts and sent them out one each weekday to everyone who had signed up to receive them. It was a huge success.

While this is effective for a church, as an individual you can highly bless people with prayer texting. Consider sending a text with an important prayer need to two or three friends. Or even better, text a prayer you are praying for someone you care about to let them know you are praying for them.

Practice

Pick a friend who needs encouragement and text them a prayer. Select a friend who is suffering and text them a prayer. Let a child or grandchild know you are praying for them today.

You know you have it when . . .

Prayer texting is normal and something you are utilizing all the time.

NOTES

_____

_____

_____

_____

_____

_____

_____

_____

CREATIVE WAY

Prayers of Grief

and Loss

So many people today are hurting and grieving because of loss. Perhaps you are, too. We know the Holy Spirit to be the Comforter. As people of prayer, we need to be ready to be agents of healing to grieving people around us. I learned to pray for grieving people with more faith because of John 11.

The resurrection of Lazarus is breathtaking. In John 11, we find Mary, the one who anointed Jesus with perfume and her sister, Martha, reaching out to Jesus on behalf of their sick brother. Jesus does not respond the way they had hoped. He does not stop what He is doing immediately and come to comfort them. He waits two more days before He begins His journey to Bethany. He tells His disciples that His actions are so that the Father may be glorified. Is it fair to say that Jesus does not always approach things or our needs the way we would?

When Jesus finally arrives notice three things:

1. His tenderness. He asks, "Where have you laid him?" and then He weeps with Mary and Martha. He enters into their pain not as a counselor but as a participant. Jesus is willing to enter into your pain also if you allow Him in prayer.
2. He calls for the stone to be rolled away despite the complications that poses.

It is heavy and Lazarus has been in the grave for four days. God is not concerned with apparent obstacles. They create no threat or hindrance to Him. He is not threatened by the hurdles you face in grief or loss, either.

3. Then He gives us a key to grief and loss. If you believe, you will see the glory of God. He was telling Mary and Martha to trust and they would see the glory of God. The same is true for us. If we believe/trust completely, we, too, will see the glory of the Father.

Based on this, here are some things to pray:
- Ask Jesus to enter your pain or the pain of the peson for whom you are praying.
- Ask Jesus to "roll away the stone" or any blockage or hindrance to healing for either yourself or the person for whom you are praying.
- Ask Jesus to show you His glory in the midst of the pain you or your friend is experiencing.

Practice

Write down the areas of grief or loss that you want to expose to the glory of the Father, be it for yourself or a friend. It will not come by holding on to them but by handing them over to God and trusting Him with their outcome. Record what you are committing to the Lord in faith and then seal your commitment with a prayer over each one. Do so each day this week.

You know you have it when . . .

You are able to bring comfort to others who are grieving and you can work through your grief and loss in a healthy fashion.

NOTES

_____

_____

_____

_____

_____

CREATIVE WAY

Praying for

Discernment

One of the powerful dynamics of prayer as we go deeper, is the truth that if we want to truly pray what is on God's heart over situations, He often shows us His purpose if we ask and listen.

If you want to shake up your small group or larger prayer gathering, here is a creative way to show people that God can and does reveal what you can pray for others.

Put your people in 2 lines facing each other, like this:

Listening Line: X X X X X X X
Receiving Prayer Line: X X X X X X X

Line one is the listening line. Instruct them to ask the Holy Spirit what they should pray for the person across from them and then listen to the Lord for anything they might get for that person.

After a few minutes of listening, have the listener go to the person in the receiving line across from them and begin to pray for the person in the receiving line.

After this, have the lines switch roles.

Have a debriefing following the practice where people can share what was prayed over them and how meaningful it was.

A Powerful Twist

After lining everyone up into two lines, have the two lines turn their backs to each other. Quietly ask the receiving line to move over to the right one space so that the person in the listening line is now listening for one person over (but they do not know it). The person in the receiving line at one end, now goes to the other end of the line.

Now give the listeners four to five minutes to seek the Lord and then, while still facing back-to-back, share what they heard for the other person. After they have shared, have them turn around. They will see that they were listening for a different person than they thought.

We have been amazed at what we have seen using this method of discerning for others.

Then have the lines switch roles. The listeners become the receivers. You will have to get creative on how you will mix up the receiving line this second time.

Practice

Try this at your next small group or gathering of friends. Jot down any interesting notes below. Learning to listen and discern is an exciting adventure.

You know you have it when . . .

You are discovering more and more ways to discern God's will as a group.

NOTES

_____

_____

_____

_____

_____

_____

CREATIVE WAY

"Washing Feet"

Prayer

In John 13, Jesus does something very surprising. He gets up from the meal and begins to wash the disciples' feet and then dries them with a towel wrapped around His waist. It was unthinkable for the Creator of the universe to do something so mundane and dirty. But, Jesus washed the disciples' feet to leave us an example of the humility and level of service that Christianity requires.

I have often thought that intercession is an act of service. At times when we really get into praying for a person or situation, we can lose track of time as we pour out our hearts in prayer. We may not realize it, but we are serving those for whom we pray.

"Washing Feet" prayer is a way to serve people for whom we do not normally pray. It is where we consciously decide, with the guidance of the Holy Spirit, to cover a unique person (someone we might not typically pray for) in regular, intense prayer.

Practice

To do this, start by asking the Holy Spirit for a person for whom He wants you to intercede. Then ask Him for Scriptures to pray and for insight into

His purposes for them. If you want to get fully immersed in this type of prayer, do it each day this week. Go through the process for seven people you want to serve ("wash their feet" in prayer) and list their names. Pray for one each day this week. (Don't be surprised if the same name comes to mind for a few days of the week.)

You know you have it when . . .
You give yourself to the intercession and well-being of others. This is the role Jesus chose when He went to heaven (Heb. 7:25).

NOTES

_____

_____

_____

_____

_____

_____

_____

_____

_____

CREATIVE WAY

Praying Your

Calendar

In this day and age, with so many things to do and great technology to keep track of everything in our lives, people keep significant calendars. They sync the calendar on their smart phone with their computer . . . and many of us also sync our calendar with our spouse's, as well.

A great practice to learn is to "Pray Your Calendar." As you look at it, why not commit to pray over the events and tasks on it?

I like to pray about events for 30 days before they happen. This isn't always possible to do, but things sure seem to go more smoothly when I do. I started praying over events more than 30 years ago, before convenient online calendars. I tried this experiment to see if events went better when they were backed by prayer. They did! So I started praying about events long before they occurred.

Now that I have a calendar that records all my "events," I can quickly pray over them with ease. Some events/tasks listed are more important than others, and God often moves me to pray more than a minute or two over them. But most are a quick prayer of blessing, or asking for wisdom, discernment, and the words to say in a meeting I am headed to.

Practice

Take out your calendar and review the major events for the next week or month. Use some of your prayer time this week to pray for each event by name.

You know you have it when . . .

This becomes a key part of your regular praying and prayer time.

NOTES

_____

_____

_____

_____

_____

_____

_____

_____

_____

CREATIVE WAY

Look for New

Opportunities to Pray

If we want to keep growing in our prayer life, often adding additional things to pray about can bring new life and refreshing to your times of prayer. We also know that 1 Thessalonians 5:17 challenges us to "pray continually." How in the world do we do that?

I think that verse speaks of having an attitude of prayer all day, keeping our eyes open and hearts ready to lift up to the Father the things that come to mind.

If we desire to pray more throughout the day, we'll start to notice that there are many occasions to pray that just pass us by. I encourage you this week consciously to look for some of those things. Here are some that come to mind:

- Weddings – praying for the new marriage and for other marriages you care about.
- Funerals – for the grieving and comfort of the family and friends.
- Before a worship service – ask God to prepare your heart.
- As a worship service is going on – that Jesus would reveal Himself to those attending who don't yet know Him.
- Brushing your teeth – That your speech was pleasing to Him today and will be more pleasing tomorrow.
- Driving a car – I use this time to thank God and worship Him.

- As you mail a letter – pray for the effectiveness of the letter.
- Doing household chores – for the chance to make your home comfortable to others.
- Moments of joy – overflow with thanksgiving.
- As you are in conversations – pray for the other person's welfare.
- Bathing children – for patience to raise them well and that they come to know Christ.
- Putting children to bed – bless them with a prayer for their future.
- Before you retire at night – confession for sins of the day.
- When you wake up – thank the Lord for His love for you and His faithfulness and ask that He would bless your day.
- As you work on the job – pray that you can be a light for the Lord at that business.
- When you pass a homeless person – pray for his or her wellbeing and help him or her if you can.
- When you pass neighbors – pray for their salvation (use B.L.E.S.S.).
- When you pass a co-worker – pray for his or her success at work (use B.L.E.S.S.).

Practice

This week look for occasions to pray. Focus on daily activities and use those simple events to remind you to pray. Jot down some of your favorite new opportunities to pray below.

You know you have it when . . .

These kinds of events automatically spark prayer.

NOTES

_____

_____

_____

_____

_____

_____

CREATIVE WAY

Make a Prayer

Album

One of my friends, Dee Duke, is the pastor of the Jefferson Baptist Church in Jefferson, Oregon. He is an amazing guy! He and his wife raised eight children. The church he pastors is almost larger than the town. People come from the surrounding areas to sit under his teaching. His secret is prayer. He is in prayer three hours a day.

One of the things he did to help him focus on prayer was to create a photo album of the members in his church and their children. When it is time for prayer, he pulls out his album and begins to call out to God for his congregation by name. The pictures help jog his memory of things he wants to remember to pray about.

Consider collecting pictures of people whom you want to pray for regularly and make an album either on the computer or the "old school" way. Then each day pray for the people you have included in your album. Make sure you leave space for notes!

Practice

Write down any revelations or insights you get using this method of prayer. Also record requests from your friends to pray over. Use that album to stimulate your prayer.

You know you have it when . . .

When you are following people through life and praying over their needs using this album.

NOTES

_____

_____

_____

_____

_____

_____

_____

_____

CREATIVE WAY

Pray for the Seven Areas of

Influence in our Culture

 number of years ago, a few prayer leaders put together a plan to engage prayer warriors in praying over all the areas of influence in our culture. They came up with seven key areas:

- Government
- Media
- Business
- Education
- Family
- Church
- Entertainment

Over the years, different groups have changed that list slightly due to their special ministry emphasis or if, in their region, there is a unique area of influence. For example, a county prayer effort in a western state added the Medical Profession as a key area of influence because they had so many companies and employees in the county related to that profession. My point is that if you see prayer guides related to the Seven Mountains or Seven Areas of Influence, while most will use the seven listed above, there might be variation in it. We are happy to see you pray for whatever area of influence the Lord lays on your heart!

Because this book is published by PrayerShop Publishing, a ministry of the National Day of Prayer Task Force (NDP), I offer prayer suggestions for the seven areas the NDP promotes: government, military, media, business, education, church, and family.

Practice

This week pray for one of these key areas each day.

For Government, you might pray things like:
- That God would give us leaders who put the nation ahead of their own interests or agenda.
- Pray for unity and not division over party lines.
- Pray for wisdom to lead through these unprecedented times.

For Military, you might pray for:
- Great intelligence to keep our nation protected.
- That the men and women who serve might find God.
- For their families while they are away.

And so on.

Come up with your own prayer items for the other areas of influence or do a Google search for "7 mountains of influence" or "7 cultural mountains of influence" and see what guides pop up.

You know you have it when . . .
You are sensitive to these key areas and they stimulate prayer in you.

NOTES

_____

_____

_____

NOTES

Join PAUL COVERT at a

THRESHOLD
Intensive Conference

The **Threshold Intensive Basic Conference** is a two-day introduction on the importance of prayer in ministry that offers practical prayer methods that will increase prayer in your church.

These methods will infuse energy into your prayer life, your church, or your organization's prayer effort.

The **Threshold Advanced Conference** is a four-day event that covers all the Threshold principles, practices and insights we have learned over the last two decades.

The **Threshold Intensive Advanced Course** is not for the faint of heart, but if you are serious about prayer, prayer ministry, and prayer leadership, this conference is just for you.

For Information: **thresholdprayer.com**

Do you want to see a greater passion for prayer in your church?

Are you equipped to be a catalyst for prayer in your congregation?

Then you need to be a member of the

ChurchPrayer
LEADERS NETWORK

The Church Prayer Leaders Network exists to encourage, challenge, inspire, and resource you as you seek to motivate and mobilize your church toward deeper levels of prayer.

Benefits of Membership:
- Annual subscription to *Prayer Connect* magazine
- Receive "Prayer Leader Online," a bi-monthly email that includes suggestions, inspiration and resource ideas to help you in your ministry of developing prayer.
- Discounts on prayer resources at prayershop.org

Go to prayerleader.com/membership or call 812 238-5504 to join.